Coaching Volleyball Beginners

Athanasios Papageorgiou
Dr. Jimmy Czimek

COACHING VOLLEYBALL Beginners

From Mini Volleyball to Volleyball: Using Games to Develop Basic Skills

MEYER & MEYER SPORT

British Library Cataloguing in Publication Data
A catalogue record for this book is available from the British Library

Original title: *Volleyball Spielerisch Lernen*, © 2007 by Meyer & Meyer Verlag

Coaching Volleyball Beginners

Maidenhead: Meyer & Meyer Sport (UK) Ltd., 2020
ISBN: 978-1-78255-202-4

Aachen, Auckland, Beirut, Cairo, Cape Town, Dubai, Hägendorf, Hong Kong, Indianapolis, Maidenhead, Manila, New Delhi, Singapore, Sydney, Tehran, Vienna

Member of the World Sports Publishers' Association (WSPA), www.w-s-p-a.org
Printed by Print Consult GmbH, Munich, Germany

MIX
Paper from responsible sources
FSC® C084279
www.fsc.org

ISBN: 978-1-78255-202-4
Email: info@m-m-sports.com
www.thesportspublisher.com

CONTENTS

PREFACE

This book was written for ***teachers at elementary to high school levels***. The first part of the book (chapter 1), which introduces ***general and specific preparatory games*** based on specific teaching methods and principles, is particularly well suited for elementary students because these "small games" can be developed in small steps that build on each other. Learning and implementing the preparatory games is the most important prerequisite for the actual introduction of the game sport (mini) volleyball.

The second part focuses on the ***introduction of 3-on-3 mini volleyball*** (see photo 1: mini-volleyball tournament) in great detail. Here, students work on each of the four basic techniques in a game setting, and under consideration of individual and group tactics via a methodical series, which consists of four learning units. The previously learned ***basic tactical serve-receive and defensive formations***, which are taught during the volleyball-specific preparatory games are amplified via volleyball techniques. The progression from ***mini to midi volleyball*** primarily serves the broadening and developing of game tactics while also serving as a reasonable transition to "big game" volleyball.

The main content of the third and final part of the book consists of "6-on-6" play with the corresponding serve-receive and defensive game formations, as well as the methodically coordinated series of ***systems of play for beginning volleyball players***.

Based on the information above, it is apparent that this book is also well-suited for ***volleyball training with children and adolescents in a school or club setting*** and is a valuable tool for the youth volleyball coach. Finally, this book is a wonderful resource for a ***physical education major in college***.

Based on the consensus that beginning training (the learning, development, and educational process) for volleyball and beach volleyball is identical, the first two chapters of this book are equally appropriate for the introduction of the game of beach volleyball.

Photo 1: Mini volleyball tournament

Organizational aids and symbols

- (circle) = Player
- (setter symbol) = Setter
- (circle with ball) = Player on/with the ball
- (dotted arrow) = Ball path thrown
- (dashed arrow) = Ball path played
- (double dashed arrow) = Ball path hit
- (solid arrow) = Running path
- (double arrow) = Shot/spin spike

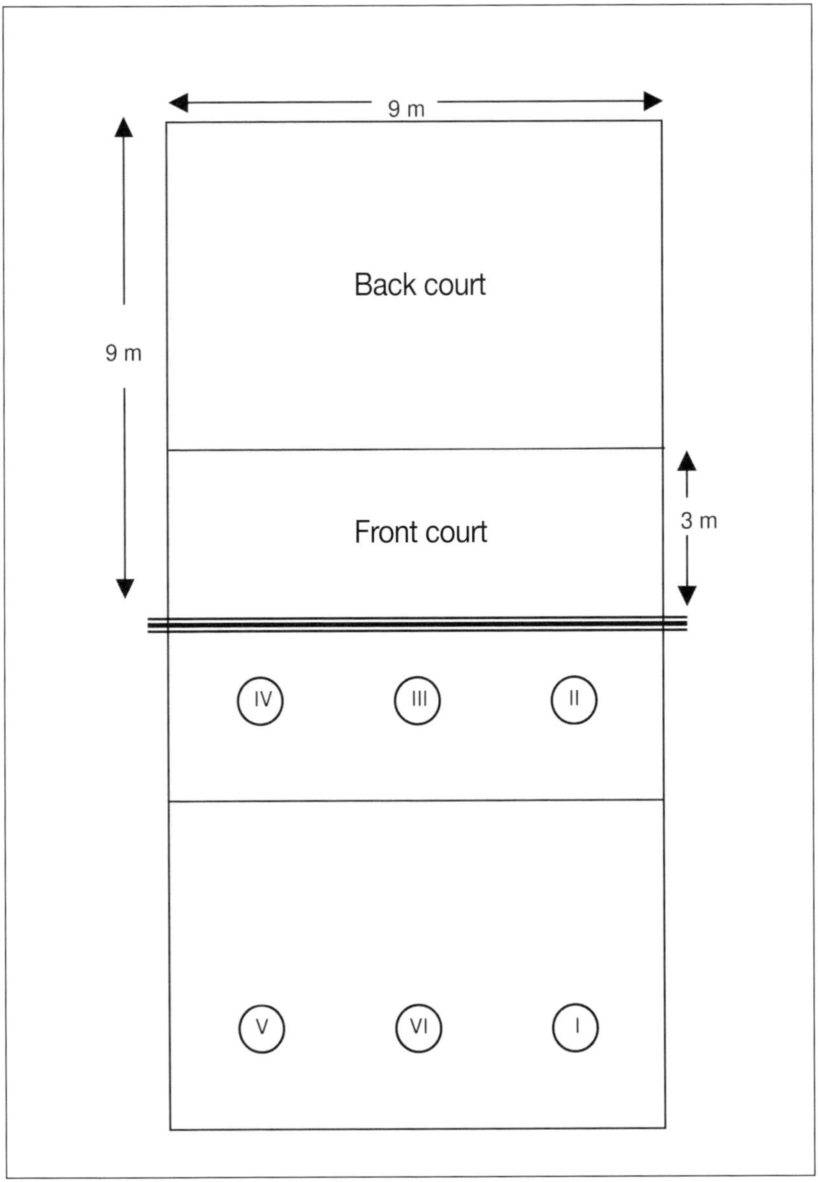

Fig. 1: Volleyball court

GAME CONCEPT AND RULES

The ***volleyball and mini-volleyball game concept*** is to play the ball over a net stretched across the middle of the court so that it touches the floor on the opposing team's half. The other team must prevent the ball from touching the floor, and keep it in the air via brief ball contacts. The ball should be volleyed back across the net with no more than three ball contacts.

Setting the ball with overhead pass (open hand contact works particularly well for beginners) and ***bumping the ball***–forearm pass–(particularly in more advanced play) are well suited for the ***first contact with the ball***. The ***second contact*** is primarily made by ***setting*** and ***bumping*** in response to bad first passes. For the ***third touch***, players can choose from several ***offensive techniques*** (shot/spin spike, feint attack/tip, spike, etc.). Several ***types of serves*** have been developed to ***serve the ball***, such as the ***underhand serve*** all the way to the ***jump serve***. The most important defensive techniques to defend against the spike include the ***block*** and the ***dig*** with its variations.

As the beginner's playing skills improve, the basic ability to keep the ball in the air develops into defensive and attacking play. The ability to receive or defend the ball (first touch) is the most important skill (prerequisite) necessary to execute an attack, i.e. an attack in the air (third touch). However, the attacking action is only possible if the first touch was accurate enough to facilitate a good set (second touch). Each team is allowed three touches for the transition from receiving/defending the ball to attacking. Utilizing these three touches is very important for creating an offensive action and the viability of the individual players or the team.

Listed next are the ***most important rules of the game***:

- A ***team*** in a big game consists of six players on the court; there are three players on the court in a mini volleyball game.
- The ***court dimensions*** are 9 x 18 m. A mini volleyball court measures 4.5 x 12 m.
- The ***net height*** is 2.43 m for men, 2.24 m for women, and 2.10 m in mini volleyball.
- ***Player positions*** are differentiated as front-row players (positions II, III, and IV) and back-row players (I, VI, and V).
- The three players in mini volleyball take up corresponding positions II, IV, and VI on a large court. There is no differentiation of front-row and back-row players.
- The player in position I ***serves*** the ball from behind the baseline.
- A receiving, defending, or setting touch is always executed with both hands. The serve, as well as the attacking ball, is always executed with one hand.
- A player cannot make two consecutive touches on the ball (except for a block).
- The ball cannot be caught, pushed, guided, or held.
- Players cannot cross the ***centerline*** or touch the ***net***. However, the ball can touch the net during every action (even the serve).
- ***Scoring*** is based on the ***rally point system***, meaning each rally results in a point scored by their own, or the opposing team. Each game consists of three sets of up to 25 points, each with a two-point differential (27:25, 29:27, etc.).
- Mini volleyball games consist of best of three sets.
- The fifth set in a 6-on 6-game and the third set in a 3-on-3 game only go up to 15 points, again with a two-point differential.
- Whenever ***service changes***, the ***serving team rotates clockwise*** by one position, meaning that the player in position II becomes the new server in position I.
- A ***point*** is awarded when the ball touches the floor, goes into the net, is out of play, when a technical execution error is made (see above), or when there is incorrect rotation or rather incorrect positioning.
- A volleyball game is overseen by a first and second referee; in mini volleyball, there is only one referee (see photo 2).

Photo 2: Referee during a competitive game

1 PREPARATORY GAMES FOR VOLLEYBALL

From a ***technical and tactical*** standpoint, volleyball is one of the ***most challenging game sports***. All of the actions that take place during a volleyball game, such as the basic elements of setting and bumping, are not based on our everyday motor functions and are therefore difficult to learn. While the major game sports (team handball, basketball, soccer, hockey, etc.) allow extended contact with the ball and the floor, as well as catching and guiding the ball, volleyball requires the playing of "volleys". This requires beginners (students) to not only make technically difficult plays and to cleanly execute movement sequences, but also ***to make the right decisions under time pressure, along with the corresponding movement skills***.

The technical and tactical aspects of the game sport volleyball are therefore particularly difficult for beginners–those cognitively not yet fully developed players with little movement experience–to learn. While all other major game sports can be introduced without preparatory games games) at the age of six, due to the flow of play not being subject to accurate execution of techniques, this is almost impossible in volleyball.

Volleyball, the only team sport with return play, only allows ***specific, very brief forms of contact with the ball*** within the scope of permitted technical executions. Hence the ***relevant mastering of basic techniques*** is essential to the precision of actions, and thus to the realization of the game objective.

Furthermore, volleyball is a ***game of errors***. Every error (for example, technically flawed play or the ball touching the ground) is immediately "penalized" with an interruption in play. This makes it all the more important to enable ***longer rallies***, particularly when the game is first introduced in order to promote joy of playing in beginners, and thereby increase motivation.

Based on the above brief outline of the structure of a volleyball game, it makes sense not to start learning volleyball-specific techniques and the game itself before age nine (3rd/4th grade). Prior to that, at the elementary school level, children should be exposed to a ***broad and general selection of all types of sports*** (gymnastics, track and field, and especially all ball game sports) in order to allow them to acquire a broad movement repertoire as a prerequisite for learning to play volleyball in particular.

Additionally, ***preparatory games/small games*** played over a period of several years are an ***essential prerequisite*** for playing the game of volleyball, as explicitly outlined below:

- Preparatory games often only require a ***small*** space but offer ***lots of intensity***.
- They require ***little equipment*** (ropes, balls, etc.).
- Many games are well-suited ***for small*** groups as well as ***large groups of children*** (entire classes).
- Preparatory or lead-up games generally ***do not require sophisticated skills***.
- They usually have ***simple rules***.
- Preparatory games are always of a ***competitive nature***.
- The ***rules of the game and the course of the game can, or must, be changed according to the learning situation*** to achieve specific educational goals.
- Preparatory games generally ***do not require a lot of start-up time*** for their implementation. They can be played after only a few explanations.

As with other major ball sports, particular attention must be paid to the methodical approach when introducing the game of volleyball, or working on advanced playing skills. This has something to do with the different mentalities in various cultures. For instance, in the Western world, we primarily use a ***methodical game series***, meaning a series consisting almost exclusively of games and competitive games, whereby Eastern European and Asian countries also successfully use a methodical ***drill series***. The methodical game series has the major advantage of motivating the learning players; however, the learning process is slower. When using the methodical drill series, the beginner ***learns faster***, but must be highly self-motivated. In our culture, we therefore recommend ***teaching by using game-like exercises instead of drills***, if possible.

Preparatory games should be versatile but should also be purposefully used to teach the skills listed below:

- ***Building strength*** (pulling and pushing games, lifting games, carrying games).
- ***Building speed*** (games of tag, foot races, relay games).
- ***Building endurance*** (relays and games requiring lower physical effort over a longer period of time).
- ***Building focus and coordination*** (obstacles and carrying relays, games with many simultaneous demands such as running, watching, dodging, or throwing).
- ***Building visual, auditory, and tactual skills***.
- ***Building awareness***.
- ***Promoting and developing social and group-tactical behavior***.
- ***Promoting creative behavior***.

It is important to note that preparatory games cannot always be allocated to just one of the items listed previously. Most of the time, several aspects apply to one game, allowing the players to have a variety of movement experiences, as well as providing students with the opportunity to acquire a correspondingly large movement repertoire.

Preparatory games for the introduction of volleyball can be differentiated as:

- General preparatory games both with and without a ball.
- Specific preparatory games (with a ball).

In addition to the athletic- or fitness-related abilities, ***general preparatory games*** also teach basic behaviors for game sports with a ball, so that beginners will learn ***ball, target, partner, and opponent behaviors that apply to all ball-game sports***.

Specific preparatory games, which are all played with a ball, are intended to specifically transition the players to the target game volleyball, ***without already incorporating particular basic volleyball techniques***. The ball should be "volleyed", meaning it should be caught and thrown without touching the floor, so the beginner can fully focus on the broadly ***occurring ball, spatial, target, partner, and opponent behavior typical in volleyball***, without having to know the specific volleyball

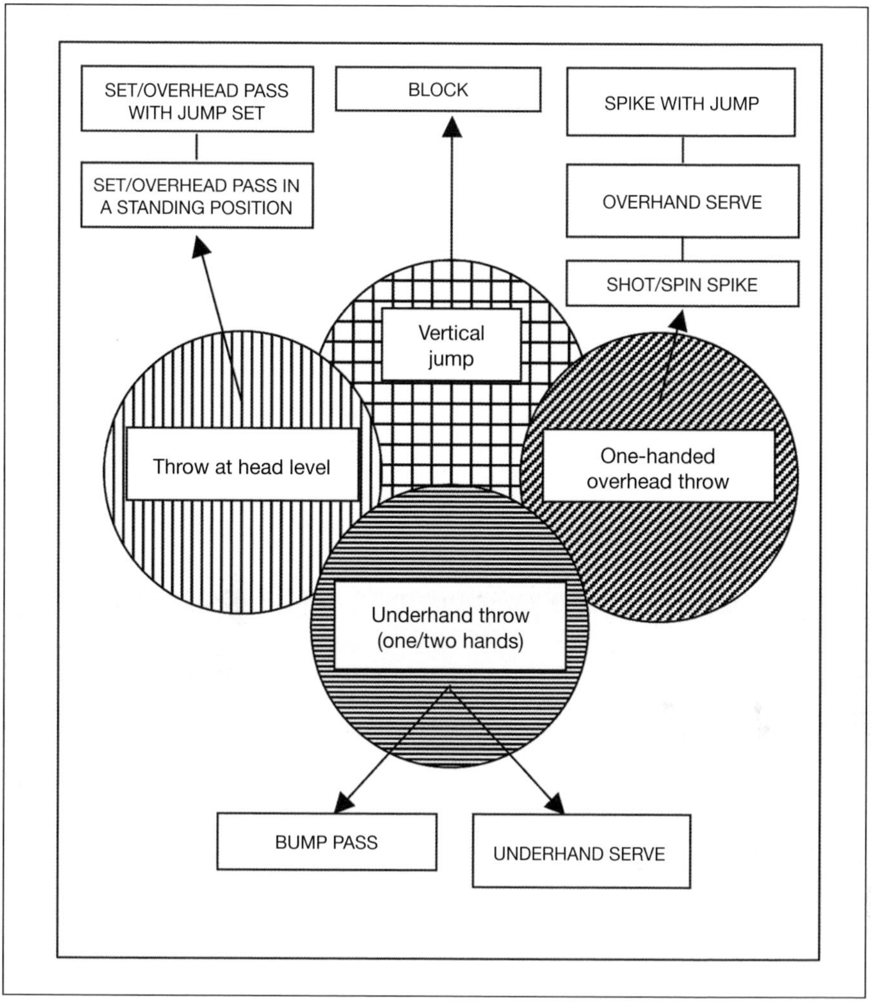

Fig. 2: Basic elements of volleyball (modified as per Zaleski, 1995)

techniques, and thus not be under time pressure. Beginners learn volleyball-like actions and the basic concept of the volleyball game step by step.

Throwing and catching games, the importance of which is illustrated by fig. 2, must be at the core of early sport-specific training. In particular, the ability to accurately estimate a ball's trajectory and then quickly assume the correct stance or position relative to the ball, represents the basic prerequisite for the subsequent learning of volleyball-specific techniques.

This previous, general, ball-based knowledge is essential for quick apprehension and anticipation of individual rallies, of more complex game situations, as well as overall playing ability or recognition of the nexuses within a game.

The basic principles listed below are also important for the introduction of mini volleyball in chapter 2.

The successful implementation of preparatory games largely depends on the ***teacher's/trainer's flexibility*** in reacting to the circumstances of a given situation, and being able to modify the games in the following ways:

- Adhering to the ***"play before drill or exercise practice" principle***: always create opportunities to compare as well as ***competitions***.
- ***Measuring the playing intensity***: create small groups and small courts with as ***many ball contacts*** for each player as possible.
- ***Paying attention to playing time***: create ***long rallies*** by creating parameters that are appropriate for the target group.
  - Vary the net height – start higher.
  - Vary the court size – start smaller.
  - Use different types of balls – start lighter.
  - Creative use of markers (e.g., sticky tape), goals, etc.

1.1 GENERAL PREPARATORY GAMES WITHOUT A BALL

The purpose of general preparatory games without a ball, which are to be played first with beginners, is to develop ***general playing ability*** (basic motor skills and general movement behavior), as well as ***general coordination skills*** (perception and decision-making, orientation ability, etc.) that are also important for playing volleyball.

Particularly important games that are based on the structure of a volleyball game are ***games*** in which children not only have to run and jump, but in addition to improving overall fitness and agility, must work on ***speed*** and ***reaction ability, acceleration*** with and without directional changes, ***stopping, contact with the ground, and lateral movements***.

The first four (1-4) examples are not games as such, but rather exercises that are introduced because they are excellent warm-up exercises. They serve to optimally prepare the body for the subsequent playing effort and thus can be a part of every training unit.

1 Changing the gait

Walking, hopping, jumping, walking on heels, walking on toes, skipping (with/without swinging the arms).

Variations:

1. Change the gait and direction of movement (forward, backwards, or sideways).
2. Spin around on command; later touch the floor with both hands and/or change the gait.
3. When they hear a clap, children lie down on their stomach/back.
4. When they hear a whistle, children "draw" a line or a circle on the floor with their hands.
5. Combination of variations (1) to (4): For example, a verbal command means changing the gait; a whistle means a vertical jump; clapping means lying on the stomach, etc.

2 Side steps

Side and glide steps to the right and left, with and without swinging the arms, and finally with nearly straight arms in a deep defensive position (photo 3).

3 Crossover side steps

Crossover steps with side shuffle: Legs cross in front and back, arms remain extended. Tempo should vary.

4 Skipping

Skip forward, backwards, and sideways with forward/backwards arm circles, also alternate the direction of movement, with opposite double arm swings and arm circles.

The following six competitive partner exercises (5-10) particularly focus on strengthening the muscles, while also working on reaction, balance, dexterity, speed, and basic endurance.

Photo 3: Side steps in defensive position

5 Tapping

Two children try to lightly tap each other on the back while trying to avoid getting tapped.

Variations:

1. Play for a certain amount of time.
2. Play in a limited area.
3. Change the target area, for instance tap only the calves.

6 Chasing feet

Two children try to step on each other's feet without having their own feet stepped on.

Variations:

1. Play for a certain amount of time.
2. Make the playing area smaller.

7 Shadow play running

Two children stand opposite each other. One moves sideways, forward and back, hops, jumps, stops, and suddenly changes direction. The partner must react at lightning speed to copy all of the movements.

Variation:

1. Shadow child (can only be played outside when it is sunny). Two children stand opposite each other. One child moves, runs, etc. The shadow child tries to stay in the other child's shadow while copying his movements.

8 Balancing competition

Two children stand opposite each other with their legs in a straddle position (legs are shoulder-width apart) and touch hands. Each tries to unbalance the other so that both feet leave the ground.

Variations:

1. Children hold on to each other with their hands.
2. Children stand back-to-back to push each other off balance.
3. Start the game in a squat.

4. These preparatory competitive games can also be played in a smaller, field with boundaries. Whoever pushes the other player off the field first, wins.
5. Starting position on one leg.

9 Touch tag

Two children compete against each other at the centerline. Each child tries to tag the opponent with a finger, and then runs away to their own baseline (approx. 9 m) so that the opponent cannot tag him inside the playing field (photo 4). Whoever is first to win 3x or 5x is the overall winner.

Photo 4: Touch tag

10 Chase the thief

Two children compete for a ball (cloth/hoop) placed on the centerline. After a signal, both children simultaneously start from the same distance (6 or 9 m) on opposite sides and try to win the ball or object. They then carry it across their own starting line without getting tagged by the opponent (photo 5). The opponent tries to take the ball or tag the opponent in possession of the ball. Feints should be used to beat the opponent.

Variations:

1. Play with several players dog-eat-dog (fig. 3).
2. Play with several players 2-on-2 or 3-on-3.

Photo 5: Chase the thief

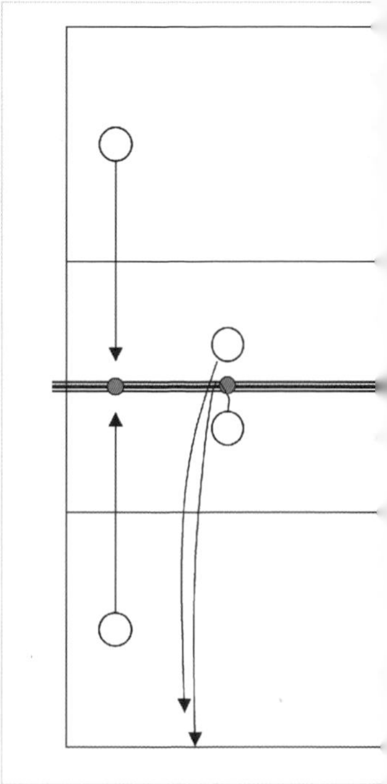

Fig. 3: Chase the thief

The following 10 competitive games (11-20) in small groups also work on partner and opponent behavior.

11 Bodyguard

The group (three children) is made up of a "star", his "bodyguard", and a "fan" that wants to touch the star. The bodyguard tries to prevent this by screening the star. The star must cover a certain distance (9 m) without being touched (photo 6). Players switch after the star has been touched by the fan, or has successfully completed the mandatory distance without being touched.

Variations:

1. Each position can be manned by multiple players (e.g. two stars, two bodyguards, and/or two fans).
2. Instead of touching the star, the fan must tag him by throwing softballs at him.

Photo 6: Bodyguard

12 Alphabet catch

Every child in each group (consisting of three children) is (mentally) assigned one letter, e.g. "A", "E", and "S". All children (all groups) run around on the field. The teacher loudly and clearly calls out a word that begins and ends with two of the chosen letters (e.g. **s**af**e**). Next, the child with the first letter ("S") teams up with his group partner with the last letter ("E") to catch the third child ("A") ("S" and "E" catch "A"). When the teacher whistles (after four, six, eight seconds), the game is over. The two catchers each get one point for catching. If the third child is not caught, he receives one point. Every child keeps track of his points.

Variations:

1. Name words that begin and end with the same letter (e.g. Anna). The child with that letter ("A") is chased by the two other children ("E" and "S").
2. The two catchers must first hold hands before they try to catch the third child (photo 7).

Photo 7: Alphabet catch

13 Caterpillar

Two to three children team up to form a caterpillar. They line up, one in front of the other, in a pushup position and then each child places his feet on the shoulders of the partner behind him (photo 8). Each group tries to cover a prespecified distance as quickly as possible. The order of the caterpillar members should change during multiple races.

Variations:

1. If the children have trouble implementing this game, have them place their hands on the backside of the person in front of them, instead of placing their feet on the shoulders of the person behind them. They should then move forward on their knees. This variation can be done with as many as six children per team.
2. The same as the competitive game and the variation, but moving backwards/sideways.

Photo 8: Caterpillar

14 Catch in one half of the court

One catcher tries to tag the other players in one half of the court (9 x 9 m). The player that is tagged, or leaves the field, becomes the catcher. The entire body is a target area.

Variations:

1. Only the thighs are a target area; subsequently only the calves.
2. On a smaller field, first players can only hop and later hop on just one leg.
3. In the gym: Players can only walk/run on the lines of the gym floor.

15 Sun – shadow catch

Children are divided into a sun group and a shadow group, whereby children from the different groups lie on their stomach in pairs, and face each other. A boundary line separates them. The trainer designates one group as catchers with a verbal signal of either "sun" or "shadow". The group that is called jumps up and sprints to catch their partners/opponents from the other group. The catching distance is approximately 9 m.

Variations:

1. The competition begins with different starting positions: on the back with feet together, on the back with heads together, on the stomach with feet together, and on the stomach with hands together, etc.
2. As above, but with different gaits: running backwards, crabwalk, crawling on all fours, one-legged jumps and standing jumps, etc.

16 Color catch

Depending on the size of the whole group, up to four catchers are designated, each one marked with a different color ribbon/shirt (e.g. red, blue, green, yellow). The catchers work as a group and try to catch the other children. In doing so, only one color at a time acts as the catcher. This player can designate a different, better-positioned catcher (i.e. color) at any time by loudly calling to him. Any player that is caught is out. The teacher must measure the amount of time it takes for all children to be caught. The catchers are then switched. *The group of four that catches the other players the fastest, wins.*

Variation:

1. The players that have been caught must stand where they were caught, with their legs in a straddle. They can only be released when another player crawls/dives through their legs.

17 Supermarket

Four teams of four to five students are each positioned on a small mat in the corners of one half of the court (9 x 9 m) (fig. 4). One basket (hoop) for each team is placed in the middle of the playing field. Each basket (hoop) contains five, seven, or nine identical objects (e.g. 10 tennis balls for one group, 10 volleyballs for another group, 10 ribbons for a third group, etc.). The goal of each group is to, as quickly as possible, transfer their group's items to their shopping cart (a second hoop placed in front of the mat). Only one player in each group is allowed to "shop"; when the object has been placed in the cart, the next player takes over. Each player can "buy" only one item per lap, however players can also "shop" the opposing group's objects. This means that players can, or must, take items out of other group's shopping carts and place them in their own cart in order to gather all of their own objects. The teammates in their own group not only watch the flow so that they can make good choices, but must communicate loudly with each other to implement the best strategy. *The first team to have all of their items in their shopping cart, wins.*

Variation:

1. Two players from each group can "shop" at the same time (recommended particularly for larger groups).

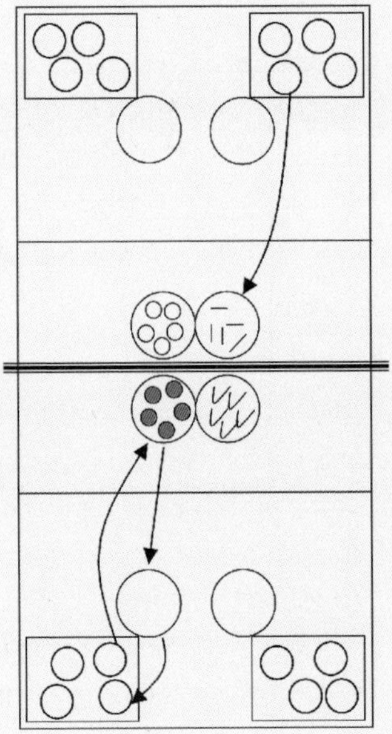

Fig. 4: Supermarket

18 Coast guard

The children are divided into "smugglers" (X) and "coast guards" (O) (fig. 5). The coast guards are lined up in two/three rows (each 1-2 m wide) and approximately 3-4 m apart, and try to tag the smugglers without leaving their posts. The smugglers start behind the baseline and try to carry tennis balls, clothespins, etc. to the other side of the field without leaving the field. Only one ball can be smuggled with each attempt. The balls are deposited into a small turned-over box behind the field. When a smuggler is caught, he must go back behind the baseline and try again. Playing time is 2-3 minutes. Next, the smugglers/coast guards switch activities. *The team that smuggles the most tennis balls across the playing field, wins.*

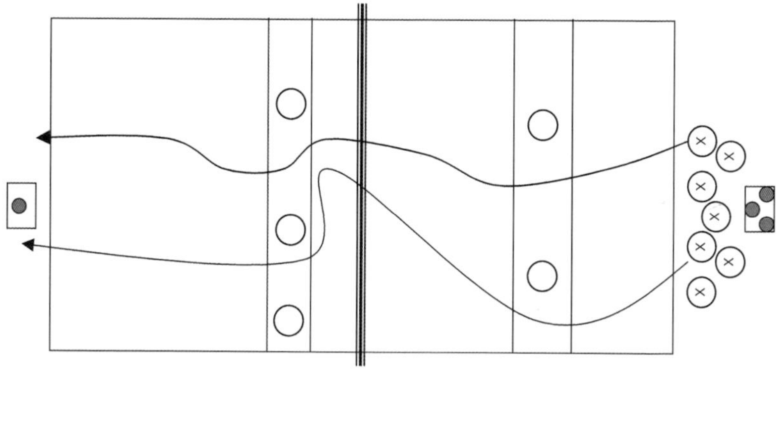

Fig. 5: Coast guard

19 The ghost of the countess ("Ghost")

Two teams (five, seven, nine children each) play against each other. Each team has a small box on the opposite side. The teacher designates a player from team A as "Ghost" (the host of the ancestors). This player must try to touch the box on the opposite side (and deposit the ghost in the box). His own team must support him (by opening up paths), and the opposing team B chases him (fig. 6-8). If a player from team B touches the "Ghost," he becomes the next "Ghost", meaning he tries to carry the ghost to their own box on the opposite side. "Ghosts" cannot re-tag each other. *The team that manages to deposit the "ghost of the countess" in the box, wins.*

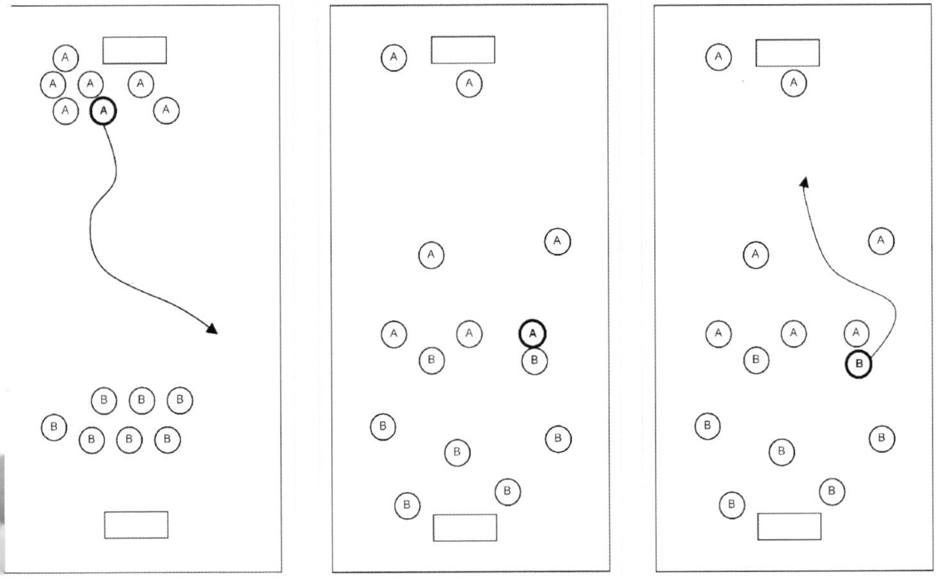

Fig. 6-8: The ghost of the countess ("Ghost")

20 (Obstacle) Ball relays

Each group consists of three or more players, and must transport a small ball in the open palm from the baseline to the net. The player then hands the ball off to his partner. If the ball drops, it must be picked up before the player can keep walking. *Which group will finish the relay first?*

Recommended action:

- Balance the ball with the arm extended!

Variations:

1. Carry a larger ball in the crook of the elbow.
2. The same game and variation, but the ball is carried with the weaker arm.
3. If one partner carries the ball with the right arm, the other partner must carry it with the left arm.
4. The same game and variations, but students must start over at the baseline if they drop the ball.
5. The same game and all of the variations, but the students cannot step on any of the lines on the gym floor.

1.2 GENERAL PREPARATORY GAMES WITH A BALL

After completing the games without a ball, the following preparatory games using a balloon, beach ball, foam ball, and other balls are introduced. ***However, the various balls used in ball game sports can, or rather must, also be used in all of the different games and competitions***.

A balloon or a beach ball is an excellent game ball for six- or seven-year-olds. Their slow flying speed makes it easier for them to anticipate their trajectory because they have more time to do so, thus making it easier to get to the ball. Practicing with these two balls outside only makes sense if it is not windy.

We start with games in which the children initially only concentrate on the ball, and later also on the partner.

21 Catch the ball

The children stand in a straddle position and throw the ball into the air with both hands, clap in front/behind the body, and catch the ball on the way down. Which child is able to catch the ball 3x or 5x in a row without a mistake? *Which child can catch the most balls in a two, three, or five minute period?*

Recommended actions:

- Throw the ball directly overhead so you don't have to move to the ball to catch it.
- Throw the ball with an extended arm or leg.

Variations:

1. After throwing the ball in the air, the children must touch the floor with both hands.
2. After throwing the ball in the air, the children should spin around once.
3. Throw the ball in the air, do a forward/backwards/sideways summersault and then catch the ball.
4. Use different starting positions for this game and its variations, e.g. on the knees, in a squat, seated, or lying down.

5. Throw the ball in the air from one starting position and catch it in a different position, e.g. throw the ball while standing and catch it sitting down.
6. This game and all variations, but the ball is tossed up from eye-level (like sitting).
7. This game and all variations (except 5), but the children jump up in the air to catch the ball.

22 Target shoot

Any kind of ball is thrown with both hands up, at a target over a line or net. The target is a circle (2 m diameter) marked on the floor (or a small mat) 3 m from the net. The net should be hung at head level. *Who will hit the circle the most in a two- or four-minute time period, or who will hit the circle 2x, 3x, or 5x in a row without any mistakes?*

Variations:

1. The ball is thrown over the net with both hands from eye level.
2. The ball is thrown with one hand from below, and later from above.
3. The ball is thrown at the target with the weaker hand, first from below and then from above.
4. This game and its variations, whereby the players throw the ball at the target from a jump, first with both hands, later with one hand, and finally with the weak hand.
5. This game and its variations, whereby the distance to the target is increased.
6. This game and its variations, whereby the target size is decreased.
7. This game and its variations over a higher net (2 m).

23 Catch and throw

Partner A throws the ball to partner B from below, initially with both hands. Partner B catches the ball and throws it back to Partner A. *Which team of two will be able to play this series the longest without any mistakes?*

Recommended action:

- Throw the ball to your partner in an arch as precisely as possible!

Variations:

1. Like the game, but the ball is thrown with both hands, and thrown and caught at eye-level.
2. Throw the ball with your back to your partner, first up and back from below, then up and back from eye-level.
3. Like the game, with the addition of the thrower having to show a number with his fingers. The catcher must call out that number before catching the ball.
4. Throw the ball to your partner through your legs while maintaining eye contact with your partner. Then do the same with your back to your partner.
5. The partners throw the ball back and forth while sitting on the floor, and later while lying down.
6. The partners throw the ball back and forth quickly and accurately while simultaneously playing a second ball back and forth with their feet.
7. This game and all its variations (except 4) over a line or a net, first at a 2 m distance, gradually increasing to 3 or 4 m.

Recommended action:

- As a ***thrower***, try to throw the ball with your legs extended. As a ***catcher***, bend your knees.

8. This game and its variations, but the ball must be thrown to the partner below the net.
9. This game and variations (1) to (3) as well as (6) to (8), however partner A deliberately throws the ball sideways to partner B so he can catch the ball in a standing position after moving.
10. This game and variations (1), (3), (7) and (9), whereby the thrower jumps while throwing the ball.
11. This game and variations (1), (3), (7) and (9), whereby the catcher jumps to catch the ball.
12. Combine variations (10) and (11), meaning both partners jump during their actions.
13. This game and variations (1) to (9), but the ball must initially be thrown ***one-handed*** with the right hand and from below, later with the left hand.

24 Keeping the ball in the air

The children try to keep a balloon or beach ball in the air with one hand, left or right, with small pushes or jabs (photo 9). *Which child will be the first to complete a designated number of ball/balloon contacts without the ball/balloon touching the floor? Which child can maintain the longest error-free series on ball/balloon contacts during a predetermined time period (two, three, five minutes)?*

Recommended action:

- ***First***, keep the ball level. ***Later***, play the ball at least 1 m into the air.

Variations:

1. Alternate hands.
2. Alternate between open palm and fist.
3. Only use the forearm, later only the head, foot, shoulder, or thigh to keep the ball/balloon in the air.
4. This game and variation (2) with both hands/both arms.
5. Every contact must be made with a different part of the body.
6. This game and its variations with different balls (softball, plastic balls, volleyball).
7. This game and its variations from different starting positions, first seated, later lying down.
8. This game and all its variations, however a predetermined distance must be completed without errors.

Photo 9: Keeping the ball in the air

25 Keeping the ball in the air (two players)

Complete game 24 "Keeping the ball in the air" and its variations in groups of two. Start with a distance of 1 m, then increase the distance to 2 m, and possibly use a separation marker (rope, net) that the ball must be played under or over.

26 What does the net do?

The children throw a ball into the net one-handed, first from a distance of 1 m, later from 2 m away, and try to catch the rebounding ball (photo 10). *Which child is able to catch the ball 3x or 5x in a row?*

Recommended action:

- Throw the ball just above the bottom edge of the net to increase its rebound trajectory from the net.

Variations:

1. Throw the ball with the weaker hand.
2. Throw the ball into the net with both hands, first from below, and later overhead.

Photo 10: What does the net do?

27 Timing games

One child throws the ball up into the air from below, and tries to catch it again with extended arms at the highest point of his jump (photo 11). *Which child is able to catch the ball 3x or 5x in a row without an error?*

Recommended actions:

- Throw the ball up high and directly above your head.
- Jump with both legs after taking a planting step (photo 12).
- Gather momentum with both arms to support your jump (photo 12).

Photo 11: Timing games: Throw and catch

Photo 12: Planting step with arm swing

Variations:

1. Like the game, but throw the ball with one hand, first with the stronger hand and then with the weaker hand. Catch the ball with both hands.
2. Like the game and variation (1), but additionally: clap your hands, touch the floor/your heels, spin around once, etc.
3. The game and variation (1) with the ball thrown slightly forward so the jump must come out of the movement.

4. ***Like the game and its variations, but the ball is not thrown in the air but instead thrown indirectly with both hands, meaning it is bounced very hard on the floor so it can then be caught at the highest point of the player's jump.***
5. Like the game and all its variations, only the ball is thrown/bounced on the floor by the partner.
6. Like variation (4), but the ball is indirectly thrown/bounced against the wall, meaning the student stands 3 m from the wall and throws the ball on the floor 1 m from the wall so the ball then rebounds against the wall and bounces back high off the ground.
7. Like variation (6), only the ball is indirectly fisted hard against the floor in front of the wall (photo 13) and the rebound is caught from a jump (photo 14).

Photos 13/14: Timing game against the wall

28 Hot ball 1-and-1

Two players stand facing each other. Player A throws the ball high and on target to his partner. Player B catches the ball and throws it back from a single jump. After five successful actions or 10 attempts, the students switch tasks. *The pair that has switched tasks 4x (i.e. successfully completed 10 actions), wins.*

Recommended actions:

- Catch the ball while it is in its ascending phase.
- Throw the ball back to your partner at the highest point in your jump or just after.

Variations:

1. Start by playing the game over a shoulder-high, and later a 2 m high net/line.
2. This game and the variation, whereby both players catch and throw the ball during a jump. Which pair can do this 6x in a row without an error?

29 Timing group competition

Play game 27 "Timing games" and its variations with three players. Two children try to first touch the ball thrown in the air by the third partner at the highest point of their jump, and later catch it. The winner of one play becomes the thrower. *The player that touches or catches the most balls in a 2- or 3-minute time period, wins.*

Variation:

1. Play the game with two players, whereby the winner throws the next ball.

30 Volley squash

Two players stand on a 3 x 3 m field bordering a wall. The players take turns throwing the ball against the wall so the opponent is unable to catch it before it touches the floor. The first meter of the wall is a so-called free zone. If a ball drops there, it is a thrower's error and one point is scored by his opponent who gains possession. Scoring is based on the rally point system. *The first player to score 15, 20, or 25 points (with a two-point differential) wins.*

Variations:

1. Players cannot move with the ball but must throw it from where they caught it.
2. Increase the size of the playing field (4 x 4 m).
3. Choose a corner of the gym (with two walls) as the playing field.
4. Play with different size balls, large to gradually smaller (volleyball, handball, tennis ball).

The following competitive games are played with three or more players to work on spatial, partner, and opponent behaviors.

31 Catcher in the middle

Two children stand approximately 3 m apart (no more than 4 m). A third child stands between the two others and is not allowed to get closer than 1 m to either one. The partners throw each other the ball underhand, using both hands, so that the child in the middle cannot reach the ball, but the partner can. If the catcher in the middle touches the ball, meaning the other partner is unable to directly catch it again, the player that committed the error must go in the middle.

Recommended action:

- Throw the ball to the partner high and on target.

Variations:

1. Throw the ball at eye-level.
2. When five or more play, the game is played in a circle with as many as two catchers in the middle, or with multiple balls (photo 15).
3. The game and its variations, but the thrower jumps when he throws the ball.

Recommended actions:

- Communicate with your teammates by calling to each other.
- Pay attention to the opposing catcher's stance inside the circle.

Photo 15: Catcher in the middle (with two catchers)

32 Team ball

Two equally large teams try to pass a ball within their own team without an opposing player touching the ball. Possession changes whenever an opponent touches the ball or the ball touches the floor, or the ball is held for more than three seconds (by a player). *The group that manages to pass the ball 8x, 10x, or 12x in a row without making a mistake, wins.*

Recommended action:

- Pass to the open teammate closest to you.

Variations:

1. The player in possession can take no more than three steps, and later none.
2. The catchers must not only touch the ball but must actually catch it.
3. This game and its variations, but without return passes.
4. This game and its variations, but the ball can only be passed from a jump.

33 Box ball

Two teams of 4 to 10 children each try to deposit balls in an opposing vaulting box/circle/hoop, located on the opposing baseline. The other team tries to prevent this by intercepting the opponents' balls while also depositing their own balls in the opposing box. Students in possession can take up to three steps. The ball can be thrown as a direct pass, or indirect as a floor pass. Each team has the same number of balls and starts behind their own baseline. Any balls deposited in the boxes cannot be taken out again. *The group that deposits the most balls in the opposing box within three or five minutes, wins.*

Recommended action:

- Whenever you are not in possession, try to move around so you can intercept an opposing ball and are also open to receive a pass from your teammates.

Variations:

1. Players in possession can no longer walk/run with the ball.
2. This game and variation (1), but the ball can only be played direct (no contact with the floor).
3. This game and its variations, but the ball can only be passed from a jump.

34 Mini Rugby

Two teams face each other at the baseline. The ball is on the centerline. When the whistle blows, the children run to gain possession of the ball. However, the player in possession can only take three steps with the ball and then must pass the ball to a teammate. The opposing team tries to gain possession by intercepting the ball to then bring it across the opposing baseline.

Recommended actions:

- Always be ready to receive the ball when your team is in possession.
- Mark an opposing player when the opponents are in possession.

Variations:

1. The player in possession is not allowed to move and must immediately pass the ball while standing.
2. The player in possession must pass the ball from a jump.
3. Like the game, but passes can only be played backwards.

35 "Kempa" game

Two teams with an equal number of players try to get into the opposing half by passing the ball to each other. A soft mat is located at the back of each half. The goal is to pass the ball to a player so he can catch the ball while jumping on the mat (photos 16/17) (one point). If the ball touches the floor or a player holds the ball longer than three seconds, the opposing team wins the right to attack. *The team that scores the most points within a certain period of time (2 x 5 minutes), wins.*

Photos 16/17: "Kempa jump"

Variations:

1. The player must ***catch the ball while jumping on the mat and throw it down on the mat before landing ("Kempa throw")***.
2. This game and variation (1), but the ball can only be passed from a jump.
3. This game and its variations, but an attack must take place within 20, 15, or 10 ball touches.

36 Caste ball

Six to eight children stand outside a circle approximately 6 m in diameter. In the center of the circle is a vaulting box, the "castle". The "guard" is inside the circle. The other children try to hit the "castle" with a ball. The "guard" tries to prevent them from doing so. *The group wins if it can score 10 hits within three or five minutes. Then a different player becomes the "guard".*

Recommended action:

- If the "guard" stands between you and the "castle", pass the ball to a teammate who is in a more favorable position than you are.

Variations:

1. Two "guards" defend the "castle".
2. This game and variation (1), but the game is played with two balls.
3. This game and its variations, but players no longer target the "castle but the "king's crown" (medicine ball, basketball, etc.), that rests on top of the "castle" (photos 18/19). *The game is over when the "crown" falls off the "castle".*

Photos 18/19: Castle ball

37 High ball

5-6 children stand close together in a circle. In the middle of the circle is a child with the ball. The child in the middle will toss the ball up high above the group while calling out the name of another player. All of the other children scatter except for the one whose name was called. This child catches the ball as quickly as possible and immediately shouts: "Stop". All players must immediately stop. The child with the ball now tries to tag another child with the ball. If the child hits another player with the ball, that player must perform three jump squats, etc. The thrower can then open the next game round. If the thrower misses, he has to perform three jump squats and the child that he tried to tag can open the next round with the ball toss.

Variation:

1. If the child whose name was called catches the ball from the air, they can start a new round by tossing the ball up and calling out a new name.

1.3 SPECIFIC PREPARATORY GAMES

38 Balls into the opposing country

Two teams face each other, each team in its own half of the gym, separated by a net/rope (2 m high). The teams start the game with the same number of balls. After a signal from the teacher, both teams try to quickly throw the balls over the net/rope into the opposing field. The game lasts one, two, or three minutes. *The team with the fewest balls in its half when the whistle blows scores one point.*

Recommended actions:

- Spread out evenly in your half.
- Always cover any spaces opening up in your half of the field!

Variations:

1. The ball can only be thrown overhead with both hands.
2. The ball must be thrown with both hands into the opposing half with the player's back to the net.
3. The player is not allowed to move with the ball.
4. This game and its variations with these additional tasks:
   a) After throwing the ball, the player must touch a line on the gym floor/a wall.
   b) After throwing the ball and touching the wall (variation 4a), the player must jump straight up, do a summersault, or a push-up.

39 Volleys into the opposing field

Game 38 "Balls into the opposing country" and its variations with six to eight players per team on a volleyball court (9 x 18 m), first with one ball and later with two. The ball thrown over the net must be caught in the opposing half. Errors are:

a) The ball lands in their own half.
b) The ball lands outside the playing field.

The team that makes the fewest errors in a two, three, or five-minute time period wins. Use two referees for better organization (each referee only counts one team's points). When playing with two balls, only count the points scored by both teams, meaning how many times each team's balls hit the floor in the opposing teams half.

Variations:

1. This game with these additional tasks:
   a) The player must touch a line on the volleyball court after each throw.
   b) The player must perform a vertical leap, a summersault, or a pushup off the field after each throw.
   c) After throwing the ball, the player leaves their own half and runs along its boundary line, along the entire baseline, and enters the playing field at the opposite sideline.
2. This game and variation (1), but the ball must be played across the net from a jump.

Recommended action:

- Before throwing the ball over the net, watch the opposing team's positioning so you can throw the ball into an unmarked zone or in between the players.

3. This game and its variations, but the ball(s) must be thrown 1x to a player on their own team so it can be thrown to the opposing team from an advantageous position.

Recommended action:

- Pass to the teammate in a more favorable position after calling out to him/ making eye contact.

4. This game and all variations, but with three to four front-row players in a 3 m space, meaning in the front third at the net, as well as three to five back-row players. The ball must now be thrown from the front court into the opposing back court. The back-row players alone are responsible for catching/defense. After successfully catching the ball, it is passed to a front-row player, who will execute the next attack into the opposing backcourt. Players switch from front-row to back-row and vice versa after halftime.
5. This game and variation (4), but the two players who participated in the pass from back-row to front-row change positions.

40 Four-field ball

Nets are set up to form a cross, to mark four equally large playing fields (each field measures 4.5 x 4.5 m). Each team has four players. They start with one ball and later throw and catch two or three balls. The teams must rotate the ball clockwise. The ball must always be thrown from the place where it was caught.

Balls that travel off the field or touch the floor are considered errors. *The team of four that scores the most points within a three- or five-minute period, meaning throwing balls to the opponent he is unable to catch, wins.*

It is recommended to use a non-playing team as referees. Each player counts the points of one of the four teams. Teams change fields after each round (three or five minutes) so that each team is continuously playing against new opponents.

Recommended action:

- First orient yourself beside the team that is attacking your field!

Variations:

1. The ball can be thrown to a teammate so he can throw the ball over the net from a more favorable position.
2. This game and variation (1), but the throw over the net must be done with a jump.
3. This game and its variations, but the direction of play is counter-clockwise.
4. This game and variations (1) and (2), but instead of circular play, the teams now attack the two neighboring teams and later also the diagonally opposed team. This variation begins with only one ball. A second ball can be added once the variation has been mastered.

"Ball over the net" games

This very important preparatory game is developed in great detail as a methodical game series from practicing with a partner or group from 1-and-1 all the way to the "3-on-3" target game.

We begin with partners, either ***one ("1-and-1"****; photo 20) or as a group of* ***four****, with two on each side ("2-and-2"; photo 21). Then we move on to games* ***against each other****.*

Photo 20: Catching and throwing with a partner "1-and-1" or "1-on-1"

Photo 21: Catching and throwing in a group "2-and-2" or "2-on-2"

Following these variations, students will transition ***to groups of six, with three on each side (3-and-3)*** *and later* ***3-on-3*** *(see photos 22-24) in an open triangle without a designated setter (see fig. 13-15). Here the students must already choose their actions and react situation-appropriate, which requires confident ball handling.*

Photos 22-24: Throwing and catching with three in a group ("3-and-3") or "3-on-3"

Eventually the game variation 3-and-3 as well as 3-on-3 with position-based attack build-up, meaning in a ***closed triangle*** *with a designated passer (see fig. 16-19), is introduced. This provides an early introduction to the* ***position-based*** *build-up as a second attack-building option in addition to the* ***situation-based attack build-up*** *(open action/game situations) (also see theoretical implementations in chapter 2).*

Methodological advice:

Children must be able to securely catch a ball approaching from a distance of 6 m as a prerequisite for implementation of the game "Ball over the net".

Organizational advice:

- If there are not enough volleyballs available, other balls, like handballs, plastic balls, or foam balls, can also be used. If there are not enough playing fields available:
  a) an additional team can stand behind the baseline on each half
  b) or individual players can stand at the ready as substitutes, either after a certain amount of time, after five points or an error. If the teams play with two/three ball touches on each side of the field, there is the option of the waiting player also rotating with their own team, or rather substituting in each time the ball crosses the net.
- ***If the rallies are too brief, it is reasonable to raise the net or make the playing field smaller.***

41 Ball over the net 1-and-1

The partners throw the ball back and forth overhand over a line/net (more than 2 m high) on a 2 m (width) x 6 m (total length) playing field, arbitrarily at first, and later ***on target with both hands at eye-level***. It is considered an error if the ball touches the floor, or a player takes more than two steps with the ball. *Which pair will be the first to, for instance, cross the net 10x or in a specified amount of time (one or two minutes) without making any mistakes?*

Variations:

1. This game, but the playing fields are 2 m apart (photo 25).

Photo 25: Ball over the net 1-and-1

2. Like the game, but the playing fields are 4 m apart.

Recommended action:

- Throw the ball with an exaggerated arm and leg extension.

3. Like the game, but playing fields are diagonally opposite; first at a short distance, eventually from a mid-distance (see fig. 9/10).

Recommended action:

- Catch the ball, turn to your partner on the other side of the net and throw the ball to him overhand and on target.

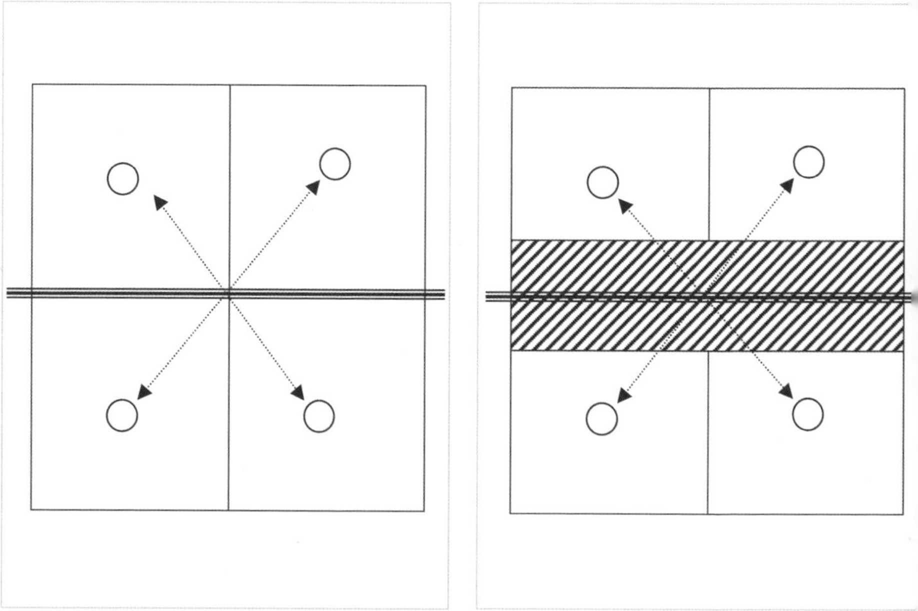

Fig. 9/10: Ball over the net 1-and-1 (on a diagonal)

4. Like the game and all of its variations, but the throw over the net to the partner can or must be accompanied by a jump.
5. The game and variations (1), (2), and (4) in "Emperor's ball" game mode (fig. 11).

For motivational reasons, it is recommended that the learning process be reinforced with tournament-style games. The "Emperor's" ball game mode, which can extend to a whole (double) class unit or training unit, is particularly well suited for all competitive "Ball over the rope" games.

Fig. 11: "Emperor's ball" game mode

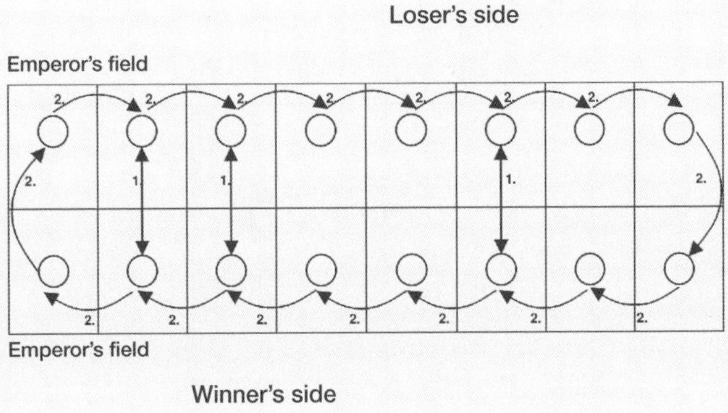

In this version of a tournament, the teams rotate on the fields after each round according to a simple principle: The winners switch to the winner's side and the losers switch to the loser's side. Next all teams rotate clockwise to the next field. The goal is to play as long as possible on the "emperor field" as "emperor", or to make it there. As a result, over the course of the tournament relatively evenly matched players or teams play against each other, which facilitates long volleys.

It is recommended to play for time (two, three, or five minutes), so that all pairs end their game at the same time. A draw will be decided by the next point.

In case of too few playing fields, or too many children, the "Emperor's ball" can be modified as follows: Players will continue to play 1-and-1, but with three players per field, meaning one player waits off the field. When an error occurs, the waiting player substitutes the player who made the error, meaning the winner of a play always remains on the field. Every player adds his points out aloud. During the big switch after e.g. two minutes, the best one of the three players switches to the winner side, the worst one to the loser side, and the player with the second most points remains on the same field, and acquires two new teammates for the next round.

42 Ball over the net 2-and-2

Like game 41 "Ball over the line 1-and-1" and its variations, but now two teams of two face each other on a 4.5 x 9 m field. Each player defends one half of their own side of the field (fig. 12). *Which group of four is the first to achieve the required number of points?*

Recommended action:

- Communicate loudly with your partner about who will catch the ball.

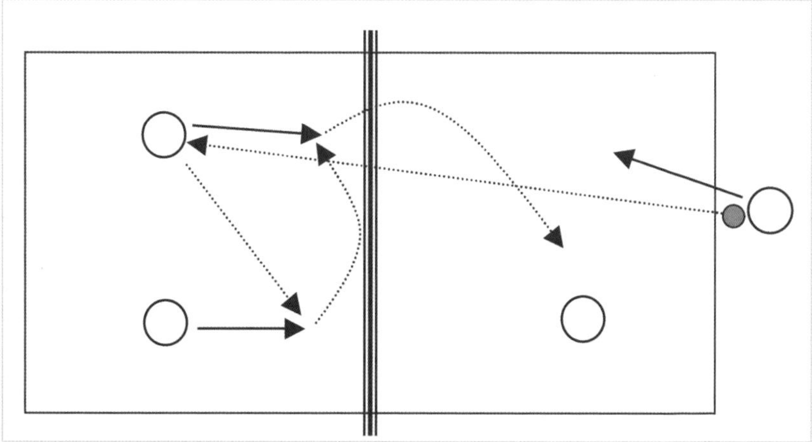

Fig. 12: Ball over the net 2-and-2

Variations:

1. At least two touches on the ball must occur on each side of the field.

Recommended action:

- Move quickly towards the net when your partner catches the approaching ball.
- Throw the ball high and on a diagonal to your teammate and not too close to the net.

2. Three touches to the ball must occur on each side of the field.
3. Like variations (1) and (2), but with these additional tasks:
   a) After the ball crosses the net, players switch positions.
   b) After the ball crosses the net, the team leaves the field and quickly runs back.

c) After the ball crosses the net, the players do a vertical leap.

4. This game and all variations, but the ball can only be thrown at eye-level and on target.

Recommended action:

- Try to catch the ball with both hands and overhead as much as possible.

5. This game and all variations, but the ball must be thrown over the net from a jump.
6. This game and all variations, but fields are on a diagonal.
7. This game and variations (1) and (5) in ***"Emperor's ball" tournament mode*** (see game 41, variation 5).

43 Ball over the net 1-on-1

Game 41 "Ball over the net 1-on-1" and its variations are played as a competitive game. The ball is thrown so it touches the floor on the opponent's side. The opposing player tries to prevent this by catching the ball. The throw-in occurs from the baseline over the net. The net height is at least 2 m. *Scoring is done via the rally point method up to 10 points, or the game is played for time (two, three, or five minutes).*

Errors resulting in a point awarded are:

a) The ball touches the floor on the field.
b) The ball lands outside the field.
c) The ball lands in the net.
d) A player holds the ball longer than three seconds.
e) The player in possession takes more than two steps.
f) The player in possession touches the net or the line.
g) A player steps onto the opposing field under the net or line, and interferes with an opponent.

Recommended actions:

- After throwing the ball over the net, move away from the net to the center of the field, and defend your field with 100% effort.
- Throw the ball into an unmarked zone on the opponent's field.

44 Ball over the net 2-on-2

Game 42 "Ball over the net 2-on-2" and its variations should be played as a competitive game (see game 43).

Recommended actions:

- Give your teammate a signal as to whether he should play a short or long ball over the net.
- Always use all three ball touches so that you can throw the ball over the net from a more favorable position.

45 Ball over the net 3-and-3

Like games 41/42 "Ball over the net 1-and-1 or 2-and-2" and their variations, however, two teams of three face each other in an open triangle (fig. 13-15) on a 4.5 x 12 x field. The player that brings the ball into the game always covers the middle and back court. *Which group of six will be the first to cross the net 10 x without an error, or have the most consecutive net crossings without an error in a certain time period (one or two minutes)?*

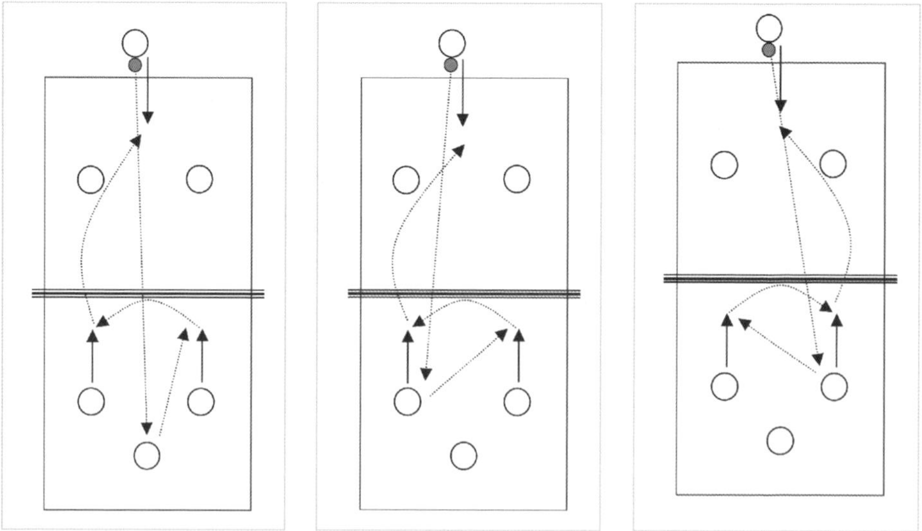

Fig. 13-15: Situation-based attack build-up in an open triangle

Variations:

1. With both teams positioned in a closed triangle (fig. 16/17).

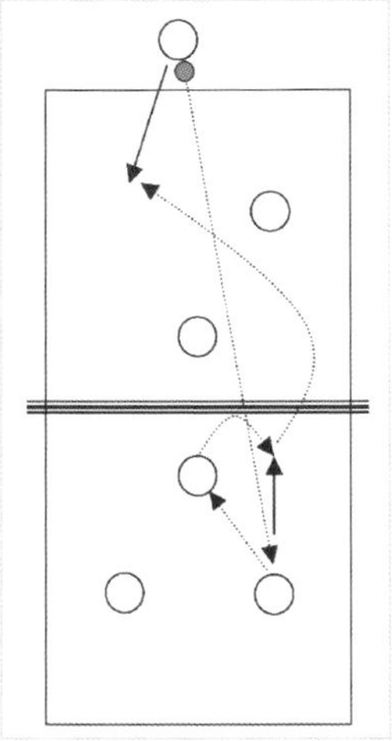

Fig. 16/17: Position-based attack build-up via position III in a closed triangle

2. Player positions in a closed triangle with the net player on the right side of the half (pos. II) at the net (fig. 18/19).
3. This game and all variations in ***"Emperor's ball" tournament mode***.

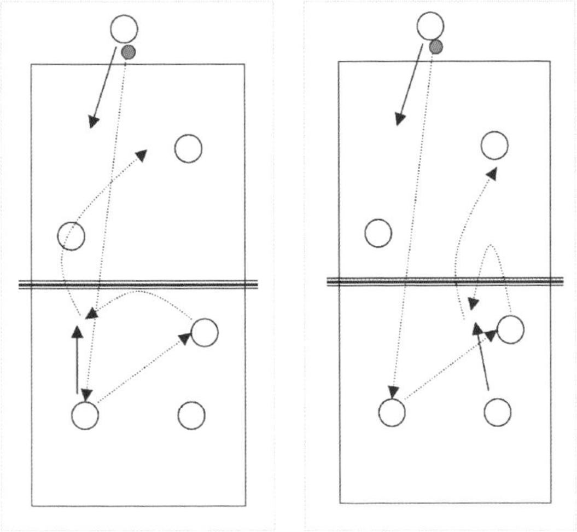

Fig. 18/19: Position-based attack build-up via pos. II in a closed triangle

46 Ball over the net 3-on-3 (target game)

Here game 45 "Ball over the net 3-and-3" and its variations should be played as a competitive game (photos 26/27). See games 43 and 44 for organization and recommended actions.

Photo 26: Ball over the net 3-on-3 (target game)

Photo 27: "3-on-3" tournament

47 Bench ball

While the game ***"Ball over the net"*** with its eye-level overhand? throws prepares players for ***setting the ball***, the game ***"Bench ball"*** introduces the basic ***bump pass*** technique. ***Like "Ball over the line", "Bench ball" also works on the volleyball player's ball, partner, spatial, and opponent behaviors and is also an important preparatory game for mini volleyball***.

A long gym bench is set up on the centerline (photo 28) with gym mats on either side of the bench, which the ball is not allowed to touch. The "mat moat" should be about 1 m wide on each side (fig. 20). Two players throw the ball to each other on a small field (3 x 6 m) across the bench and mats, in such a way that the opponent cannot catch the ball. ***The ball must always be thrown up and forward underhand with both arms below shoulder-level, and with arms extended over the bench and mats***.

Photo 28: Bench ball

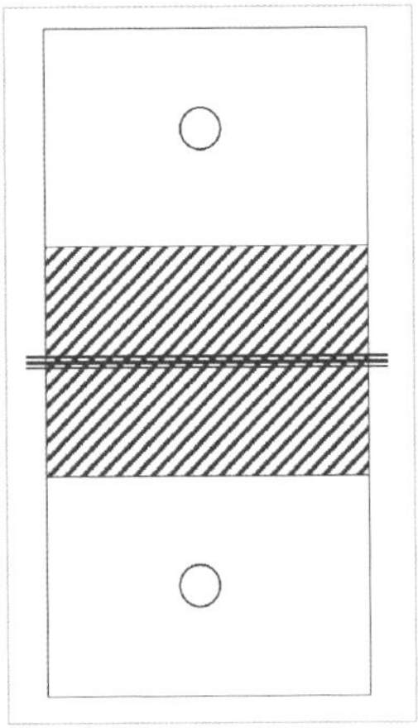

Fig. 20: Bench ball

The bottom edge of the net (approx. 1 -1.2 m) or a rope/line stretched across at the same height prevents the ball from being thrown higher. The rules of the game are the same as "Ball over the line". Catching the shallow ball and throwing the ball shallow with both hands are largely consistent with the basic underhand set/pass technique (defensive posture). The movement toward the ball is also similar to the bump.

Errors resulting in a point being awarded are:

a) The ball touches the floor on the field.
b) The ball lands outside the field.
c) The ball falls into or touches the mat moat.
d) The ball goes in the net.
e) A player holds the ball longer than three seconds.
f) The player in possession takes more than three steps with the ball.
g) The player in possession steps on the mat moat.
h) The player does not throw the ball underhand with arms fully extended.

Variations:

The competitive game series of the "Ball over the line", meaning games 43, 44, and 46 with all their variations should be completely transferred to the game "Bench ball", ***with the exception*** of the 3-on-3 variations with position-based attack build-up. ***The "Emperor's ball" game mode also works very well for the game "Bench ball".***

Methodological advice:

If the rallies are very short in the game "Bench ball", it is advisable to first play the game "together", and/or make the moat longer and lower the bottom edge of the net/line to 1 m.

Didactic advice:
Since the basic setting technique in (mini) volleyball is clearly more important than that of bumping (i.e., particularly for beginners), more time should be spent on the game "Ball over the net" by primarily preparing overhead passing and setting , instead of the game "Bench ball" which focuses on underhand passing. Nevertheless, for reasons of variability and motivation, both games can be taught nearly simultaneously/alternately. However, there should always be clear emphasis on the game "Ball over the net". An example could be that after introducing game 43 "Ball over the line 1-on-1" and its variations, the transition can be made to the game "Bench ball 1-on-1" before introducing the game "Ball over the net 2-on-2", etc.

A systematic and playful introduction to mini volleyball can easily be made via the above concept. The transition to mini volleyball should happen once the children are able to reliably catch a ball from a distance of 6 m, which means that age 9-10 should not be the determining factor for the introduction of mini volleyball.

2 INTRODUCTION TO MINI VOLLEYBALL AND VOLLEYBALL ON A SMALL COURT

Mini games, especially in volleyball, ***are the result of didactic considerations*** in terms of how big game sports can be adapted to the beginner's learning level and ability, by creating a simplified but game-appropriate learning situation that matches the beginning player's developmental stage.

Mini volleyball is derived from the game sport volleyball. It is based on the three ***didactic principles***

- from easy to difficult,
- from simple to complex, and
- from familiar to unfamiliar

as well as the number of players, the size of the field, the height of the net, and possibly the playing device change. However, the volleyball game concept, the game situations and interconnected actions, as well as the basic rules of the game sport volleyball are retained in consideration of educational principles.

The didactic principles listed above should ideally be ***combined with*** the following ***methodic-didactic principles:***

- As game-like as possible
- As simple as possible
- As often as possible
- As fast as possible

The learning prerequisites for mini volleyball have been acquired systematically and purposefully during the first part of the book so that typical game behaviors, and to some extent even ***volleyball-specific ball, spatial, target, partner, and opponent behaviors*** can now be required, and next will be refined. The goal is to work on and learn the basic elements of mini volleyball (set, bump, shot/spin spike, and underhand serve) via methodical game series, each consisting of four learning units.

The recommended games in the learning units are ***built exclusively*** and systematically on the principal of a ***methodical game series***.

The concept of the game sport (mini) volleyball involves ***two levels***, both of which depend on the level of development of the children's playing behavior:

First level:	***Keeping the ball in the air.***
Second level:	***Playing the ball over the net into the other field.***

These two levels also apply to the big game sport of volleyball and, taking into account the attack build-up, can be separated into two ***basic situations***:

First basic situation:	***Receive/defend and pass*** (First touch)
Second basic situation:	***Set and attack*** (Second and third touch)

The concept introduced here as part of a playful introduction to mini volleyball initially offers games for beginners that primarily develop the first level of the game concept, meaning the ***first basic situation*** of keeping the ball in the air. This didactic choice increases the beginner's playing intensity, the flow of play, and the joy of playing. Placing more emphasis on the first basic situation than the second is based on the following principle: ***The quality of the receiving and defensive action determines the quality of the attacking action!***

The playing ability that is a prerequisite for the playing experience and joy of playing, even in beginner volleyball, can only be acquired if the learning of defensive behavior is clearly prioritized over attacking behavior. ***Thus beginners who are able to keep the ball in the air during the game with both their receiving and defensive behavior are considered fit to play***.

For this reason, mini volleyball includes many but not all of the game situations or techniques found in a volleyball game. For instance, ***the spike is not taught***. The ball can only be played as a shot/spin spike because, on the one hand, it is easier to implement in a game since it can also be played from a standing position and on the other hand, it is easier for the opponent to reach, meaning to defend. Compared to the shot/spin spike, the spike is much more difficult to learn and most often results in lots of self-caused errors. In addition, it is considerably more difficult to defend, resulting in game interruptions along with decreased joy of playing.

As a consequence, learning the basic element "block" can be and should be skipped because the shot/spin spike can be defended without a block. The element "block" as well as expanded attacking behavior, and the resulting improved ball, spatial, and partner behavior will be the focus of the continuation of mini volleyball to the game of volleyball (see chapter 3). It is the difference between the ***competitive mini volleyball game***, which is played by international rules and requires the block as well as the attack hit, and mini volleyball as it is introduced here (see chapters 2.5 and 2.6).

It should be emphasized once more that in beginner's volleyball, all ideas that would facilitate long rallies should be taken into consideration since that is the most important factor for the learner's ***joy of playing***.

Teaching the basic techniques marks ***the beginning of mini-volleyball training***. Here, ***overhead pass (setting)*** should be introduced as the first receiving and passing technique. The new rule changes (permitting the double-hit when receiving an overhand pass) also support this school of thought. As soon as students have somewhat mastered setting as a receiving and passing technique, they will be introduced to the ***bumping (forearm pass) to encourage alternative actions during receiving and defensive situations right from the start, and provide opportunities for decision-making***. Bumping increases the beginner's range of actions. This is reinforced by allowing one-handed actions in emergency situations in terms of overhead and forearm passes, whereby the following guideline regarding accuracy and thus facilitation of longer volleys must always be observed:

Two-handed actions before one-handed actions and setting before bumping!

The ***introduction of the underhand serve*** recommended by many authors as the third learning technique is absolutely viable. This concept, however, teaches the serve as the fourth basic element since it frequently leads to errors, particularly in games on small fields, and thus to game interruptions. Until it is officially introduced, the serve should be done via a throw-in or by ***setting the ball into the game***. Instead of the serve, the ***third element*** to be taught should be the ***shot/ spin spike***, an attacking technique with a jump. While it can also be played from a standing position, the shot/spin spike should be used as early as possible with the jump as it promotes timing, which is essential for all jumping actions in volleyball and has a motivating effect on beginners. This also applies to attacking actions as overhand sets from a jump.

Only the fourth and final methodical series focuses on the introduction of the ***underhand serve***. It is easier to do and more accurate than the overhead serve, as well as being much easier for the receiving player to set. This didactic decision also increases the playing intensity and motivation of beginning players.

Tactical training, which takes place parallel to technical training and is of equal importance, in all game-like series about individual technical elements should be taught as ***1-on-1 and 3-on-3 receiving formations before 2-on-2***, because 2-on-2-play is more difficult with respect to the attack build-up, as well as communication between players.

It is extremely important to bring students into ***game situations in which they have to choose their action***, meaning game situations that have at least two solution options and thereby initiate ***decision-making processes***. That is why in beginner volleyball, ***situation-based attack build-up*** is preferable to ***position-based attack build-up*** (where passing position and passer are predetermined from the start). During ***situation-based attack build-up***, the player decides which position or which teammate to pass to, depending on where the ball is received and defended in a given game situation. Therefore, the beginner must always anticipate having to perform the first and third or the second touch. In doing so, the player is faced with different game situations from the start and must choose between different potential solutions. Consequently the ***situation-based attack build-up*** is taught first and very intensively, on a small field/mini volleyball 3-on-3 (open triangle with 3 players, fig. 21/photo 29), as well as in midi volleyball 4-on-4 (open semi-circle with four players, fig. 22/photo 30), and when introducing 6-on-6-play (W-formation with six players, see fig. 23).

Fig. 21/photo 29: Three players in an open triangle formation

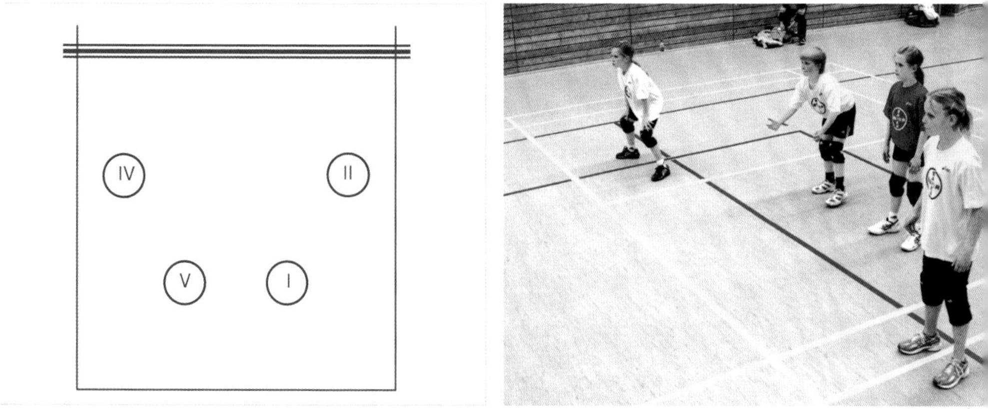

Fig. 22/photo 30: Four players in a semi-circle formation

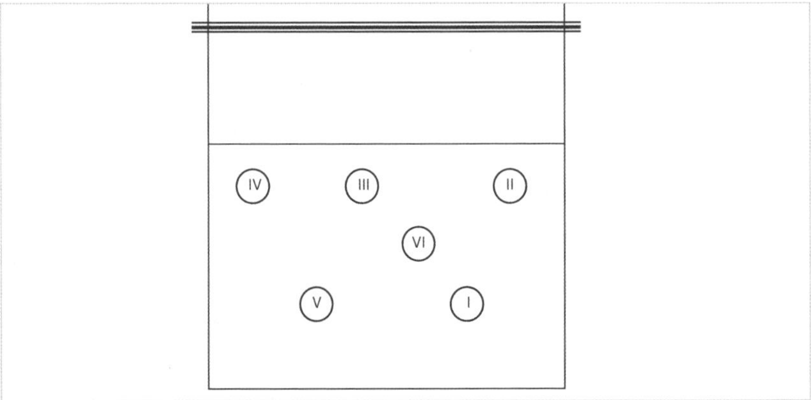

Fig. 23: Six-player defensive W-formation

According to the above statements, the situation-based attack build-up meets the four basis requirements that should be considered when introducing the game of volleyball:

- Promoting volleyball as a ***game of movement*** (running and jumping game),
- Promoting ***action and decision-making skills***,
- Promoting ***anticipation skills***, and
- Promoting ***communication skills***.

Furthermore, delaying position-based attack build-up is also justified because it requires all players to have the ability to accurately receive/defend, and pass the ball, which is very difficult to implement, particularly for beginners, and tends to lead to lots of game interruptions. Also, with the exception of the setter, the players are usually not ready for the second touch and will not accept imprecise passes in their vicinity. Due to the established procedure, they anticipate accurate passes and are not prepared to adjust to game situations that deviate from their action pattern. ***More specialized formations such as position-based and later person-based attack build-up should only be introduced after accuracy of movement and action has improved. They require specific and planned interactions.***

Aside from a reasonable succession of contents, the most important teaching variables are the ***playing experience*** and ***preserving the joy of playing*** as well as the interplay of the affective dimension and the motor, cognitive, and social dimension. For that reason, this teaching concept puts into practice ***learning to play by playing***. The playing method, meaning learning via ***game series***, is used for every learning objective and learning unit. Drill series should be used for very complicated action sequences, such as the spike.

Non-competitive and competitive games played on small fields are particularly well suited for ***game series***. ***Non-competitive games on small fields*** teach playing and movement accuracy (technical and motor skills) under simplified conditions. ***Competitive games on small fields*** teach the game-appropriate application of technical and tactical skills in the two basic situations, and develop competition-oriented behavior in terms of acting and reacting.

Playing ***1-and-1 (non-competitive)*** and ***1-on-1 (competitive)*** is particularly important with respect to technique and individual tactics. In this game, the beginner gets the most touches and thus the highest playing intensity.

The ***field dimensions*** should not be seen as standard, but should continuously be reviewed and modified according to the different playing levels. An important factor when choosing a field size is the technical/tactical action the game will focus on, or how the same can be "forced". For instance, a wide and short field puts the focus on the players' lateral and pivoting movements; a long and narrow field promotes forward and backwards movements.

If the beginners' performance level necessitates lots of simplifications to implement small-field games under easier conditions (catching the ball as well as varying the net height and field dimensions, etc.), it does not make sense to allow double plays, meaning one player can set the ball twice overhand, because the ideal position to the ball should be different. For beginners, this is difficult to do. Thus double play lures the player into assuming a playing position to the ball that is not ideal, and should only be allowed in exceptional cases. By contrast, catching the ball and then setting and passing that same ball is a promising methodical step that unfortunately does not have quite the same motivating effect on older students, since it interrupts the ball's "volley".

JOOLA
0
1

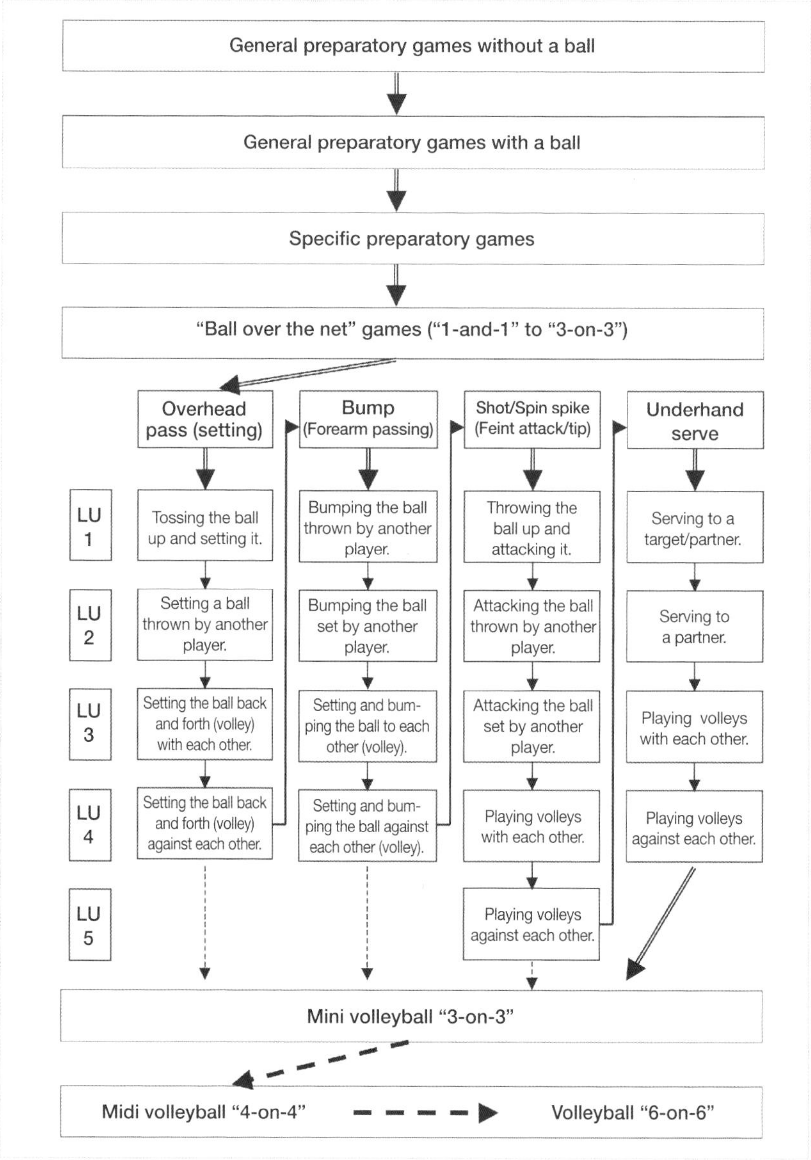

Fig. 24: The mini-volleyball teaching model

The following statements explain the mini-volleyball teaching model shown above (fig. 24). The methodical series to introduce the individual basic techniques, which vary only slightly from element to element, are briefly outlined here:

A methodical series consisting of four learning units is used to teach the ***overhead pass (set) as the first basic technique***.

The ***first learning unit***, throwing and then setting the same ball, teaches overhand passing via the easiest games. Since receiving the ball and playing it on with a very brief touch is difficult for many children, they will first catch the ball and then toss it up themselves, thereby playing a ***self-set*** ball.

In the second learning unit (***setting a ball thrown by someone else***), another player accurately throws the ball, which is essentially a simplified version of volleyball. The difference between the first and second learning unit is the longer trajectory, as well as the faster arrival speed of the ball that needs to be set.

In the third learning unit, (***setting volleys with each other***, e.g. 1-and-1) players on both sides of the net form one group and play against all of the other groups. Here, too, the game situation is still very much simplified because the children are supposed to make every effort to accurately set the ball to the player on the other side of the net.

Only in the ***fourth learning*** unit do students set the ball back and forth competitively in volleys, without catching the ball or the partner throwing the ball. Beginners must try to outplay their opponents to score points.

The methodical approach to teaching the ***second basic technique, the forearm pass (bump)*** is slightly different from that used to teach setting, as well as the skills acquired with it.

This approach skips the methodical step of students throwing the ball for themselves because it is difficult to accurately "self-set" the ball for the bump, and leads to a faulty technical execution.

The ***first learning unit*** thus begins with the ***partner*** accurately ***throwing the ball***.

The ***second learning unit*** also includes more practice of the overhand pass. Here the ball ***set by another player***, which can be assumed to be less accurate, can be returned as a forearm pass in the form of a bump.

According to the methodical approach for setting, in the ***third and fourth learning units*** students should ***play volleys with each other*** and ***later against each other***. Here, both of the previously learned basic techniques find situation- and game appropriate application. Particularly when playing against each other, players gradually use the overhead ***two-handed feint attack*** from a jump.

The shot/spin spike (***and the feint attack/tip***), which takes center stage next as the ***third basic technique***, should be learned in five methodical steps.

While students play again with the ***"self-set"*** ball in the ***first learning unit***, during the ***second*** and ***third learning units***, the attack initially comes after a ***ball thrown by another player*** and later from ***a set ball***.

The ***fourth*** and ***fifth learning unit***, games that use shot/spin spike ***volleys with and against each other***, are also based on the aforementioned principles.

The methodical step to introduce the ***underhand serve***, the ***fourth basic technique***, is very different from that of the other techniques.

During the ***first learning unit***, the ***underhand serve*** is played on ***specific targets***, and in the ***second learning unit*** it is ***played to a partner*** to facilitate lots of repetitions.

In the ***third*** and ***fourth learning unit***, the underhand serve is subsequently integrated into ***volleys with or against each other***, so children will have mastered the game of mini volleyball by the time teaching of this sub-goal has concluded.

Next, the competitive game ***mini volleyball played by international rules*** is introduced and additional elements are presented to create a transition to midi volleyball and 6-on-6 play.

Methodic-didactic recommendation:
When working on the various basic techniques, children should initially focus only on the three most important characteristics of each basic element. Experience shows that offering only two to three brief and concise recommendations on possible actions, regarding the most important movement characteristics, allows students to learn the very difficult movement sequences of volleyball techniques more quickly than detailed descriptions. Moreover, these three movement characteristics can easily be repeated and corrected again and again, making it easier for the beginner to internalize them.

2.1 OVERHEAD PASS (SETTING)

The three most important movement characteristics include:

- Body-ball relationship: ***"Hands form a triangle in front of the forehead"*** (photo 31).
- Target area: ***"Play the ball with all fingers and tension in the fingers"*** (photo 32).
- Initiation: ***"Whole-body extension"*** (from a slightly hunched posture, extend both arms and legs to move towards the ball) (photo 33).

Photo 31

Photo 32

Photo 33

Photo series 34: Movement sequence for setting (from the side)

Photo series 35: Movement sequence for setting (side/front)

First leaning unit: Setting the self-set ball

1 Setting

Each player has a ball and moves freely around the gym with it. In doing so, the player tosses the ball in the air, sets it, and then catches it. Which player will be the first to do this 5x (10x, 20x) without the ball touching the floor?

Recommended actions:

- Accurately throw the ball approximately 1 m into the air, underhand with both arms.
- Raise your hands above your head.
- Before touching the ball, get in a slight crouch with legs in a straddle.
- Set the ball with all 10 fingers.
- Your thumbs point towards the tip of your nose, and your hands form a triangle.
- Make sure there is tension in your fingers.
- Extend your body towards the ball.

Variations:

1. Set the ball toward an elevated target (marking on the wall, basketball backboard, basketball hoop).
2. The student stands close to the net in the attack zone and sets the ball over the net towards a larger target (mat, hoop) in the opposing attack zone.
3. Like (2), but the player stands close to their own attack line.
4. Like (2), but the player sets the ball towards larger targets mid-distance in the backcourt.
5. (1) to (4): The size and distance of the targets should gradually change; first larger targets at a greater distance, then smaller targets from a short distance, later mid-distance, and finally longer distance.

All variations should be executed as individual or group competitions. Which player or group will hit the target the most during, e.g. 10 attempts?

2 1-and-1 play

Two players "self-set" a ball and then set it over the net in a small field (2 x 6 m). *Which team of two will manage the longest volley within a predetermined amount of time (two or three minutes), without leaving the field and/or without the ball touching the floor?*

Variation:

1. With three or more players as a line (3-player minimum) or triangle game (4-player minimum): Each player chases after his pass (fig. 25/26).

Recommended action:

- Playing in a triangle: Catch the ball, turn in the passing direction, self-set the ball and then accurately set it to your partner.

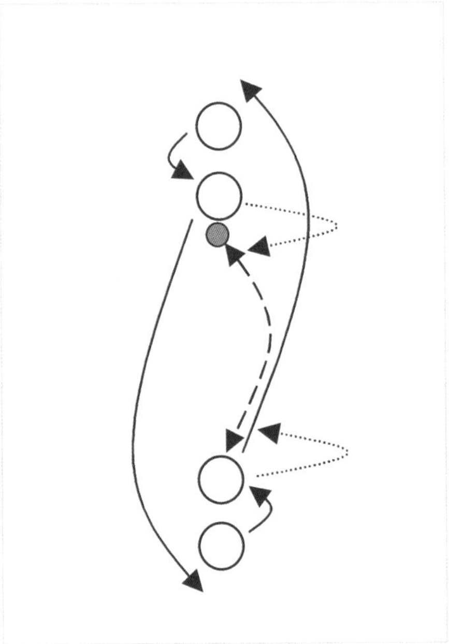

Fig. 25: Setting 1-and-1 as a line game

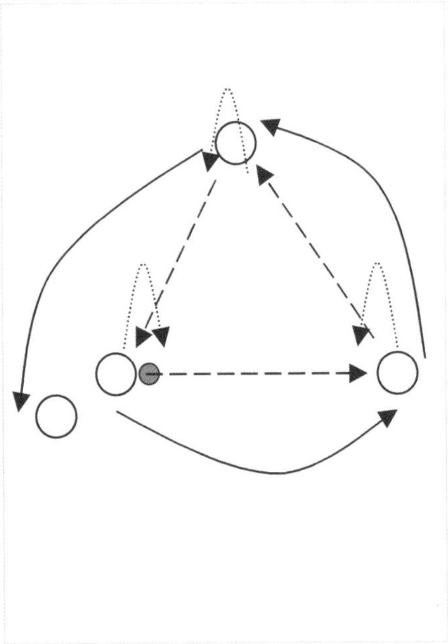

Fig. 26: Setting 1-and-1 as a triangle game

3 3-and-3 play

Two teams of three face each other in an open triangle (see fig. 13-15). Each side must complete three mandatory touches. When an error is made, the players rotate. *Which group of six can complete the highest number of net-crossings during a predetermined amount of time, without making any mistakes?*

Recommended actions:

- Stick to the specified ball and running paths.
- Always set the first ball diagonally, high, and at least 1 m from the net.
- Always set the second pass parallel to the net and high.
- Practice timely communication by loudly calling to each other, particularly with actions in overlapping areas (fig. 27/photos 36/37).

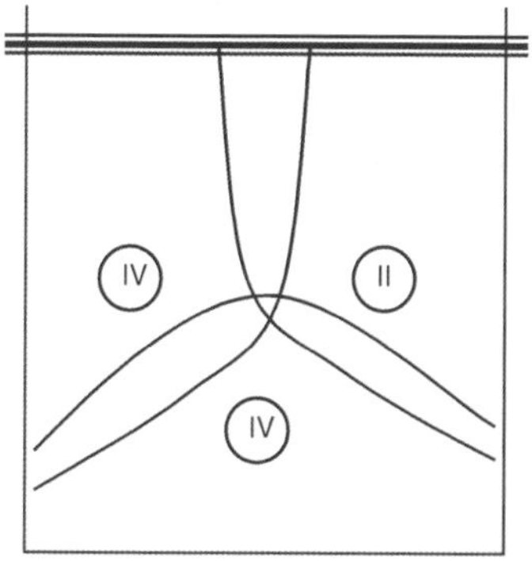

Fig. 27: Overlapping areas with three players

Photos 36/37: Communication during balls in an overlapping area

Variations:

1. Players rotate one position each time the ball crosses the net.
2. This game is played in a closed triangle formation (see fig. 16/17). The player at the net is in the middle in pos. III and should play every second touch.

Recommended actions:

- The player in pos. III should stand at least 1 m from the net so his teammates do not throw the ball too close to the net and cause him to touch the net/commit a consequential error.
- The player in pos. III should turn early or on time into passing direction, meaning just ***before*** touching the ball.
- The player in pos. III shares responsibility for receiving balls that are played very close to the net (fig. 28).
- ***Players in pos. IV or II should move at least 2 m away from the net as soon as the ball has been passed to the other side.***

3. Like (2) but to pos. II with the player at the net (see fig. 18/19).

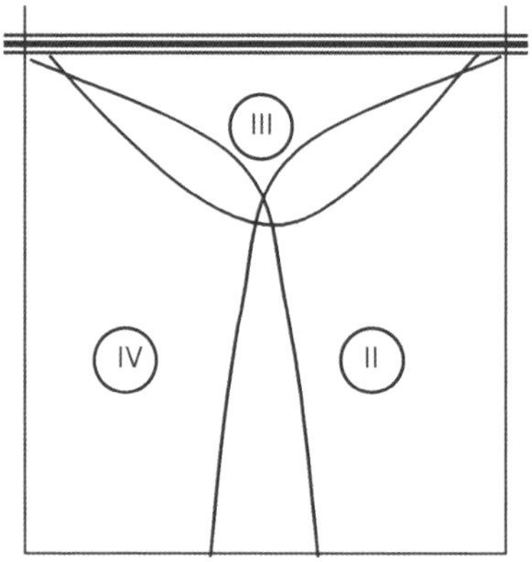

Fig. 28: Overlapping areas with two-player defense (setter in pos. III)

Recommended actions:

- The player at the net should call out loudly when he gets ready to set the ball.
- With respect to the overlapping areas, all three players communicate loudly and clearly about who should receive the ball (fig. 29/38).

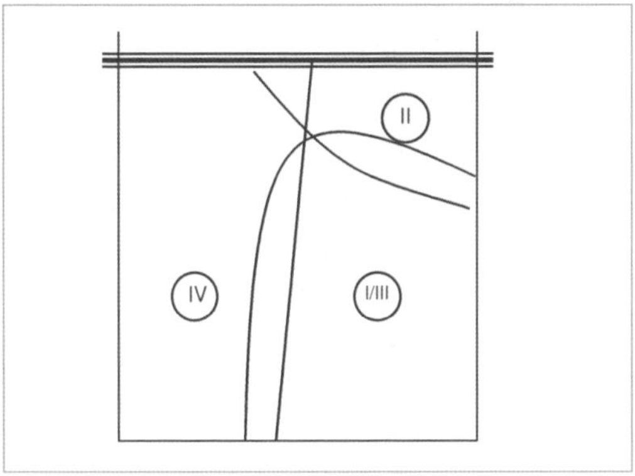

Fig. 29/photo 38: Overlapping areas with two-player defense (setter in pos. II)

4 2-and-2 play

Two teams of two stand facing each other (photo 39 and see fig. 12). Each side must complete three mandatory touches. *Which group of four will manage the longest rally within a predetermined amount of time (or 10x, 15x, etc.), without making a mistake?*

Recommended actions:

- Don't play the first pass too close to the net, meaning at least 1 m distance from the net.
- Always set the first pass high and diagonally to the net.
- Always set the second pass parallel to the net.
- Remember to immediately run to the net if you are not the one catching the ball.
- Call out to your partner that you will expect his pass at the net.

Variation:

1. Players change positions each time the ball crosses the net.

Photo 39: Setting 2-and-2

5 1-on-1 play

Two players play the "self-set" ball over the net against each other on a small field (2 x 4 m). It is considered an error when the ball goes off the field, into the net, or touches the floor, meaning not catching the ball is counted as an error. *Scoring is based on the rally point system up to 15 or 25 points.*

Variation:

Vary the size of the small fields ***based on performance level***. Start with 2 x 4 m; later go to 2 x 6 m, and finally 3 x 6 m.

6 3-on-3 play

Like game 3 "3-on-3 play" and its variations, but against each other (photo 40, see game 5 "1-on-1 play"). The court size is initially 4 x 8 m, and later 4.5 x 9 m.

Photo 40: Setting 3-on-3 in an open triangle

7 2-on-2 play

Like game 4, but against each other (see game 5 "1-on-1 play").

The field size is initially 3 x 6 m, and later 4 x 8 m.

Organizational recommendation:

All of the aforementioned games should be played against each other, and their variations should be played according to the "Emperor's ball" game mode (see chapter 1.3, fig. 11).

Second learning unit: Setting a ball thrown by another player

8 1-and-1 play

One of the players throws the ball in an arc to the other player (over the net) at head level. The partner sets the ball back so that the thrower can catch it. After setting the ball five times, the players switch. *The pair that sets the ball 10x, 20x, etc. without the ball touching the floor, wins.*

Recommended actions:

- Throw the ball to your partner underhand, high and on target, with both hands!
- Watch the approaching ball's trajectory!
- Take small steps to get underneath/behind the ball.
- Sprint as fast as you can and then slow down.
- Stop before you touch the ball.
- Stretch your body up and forward towards the ball.
- Play the ball by using your arms and all your fingers.
- Pay attention to your hand position and the tension in your fingers.

Variations:

1. 1-and-3 play: The single player alternately throws the ball to one of the three players standing one in front of the other (fig. 30), and later to the players standing next to each other (fig. 31). The receiving player returns/sets the ball as accurately as possible. *If the single player does not catch the ball, the players switch places.*

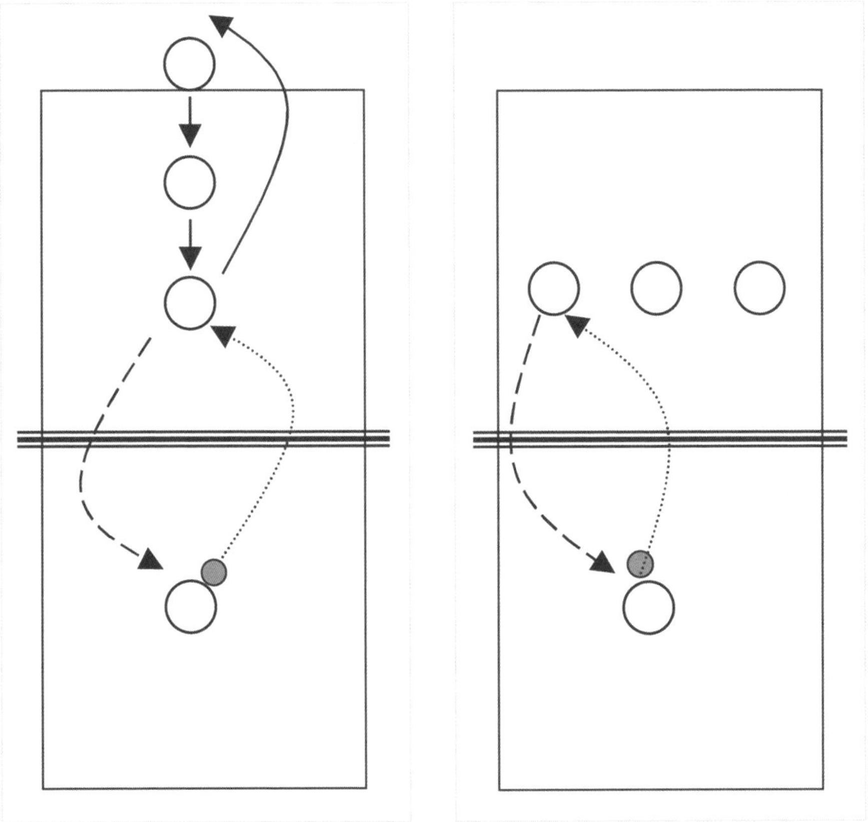

Fig. 30/31: Setting 1-and-3

2. The ball is played back on a target in the opposing field (mat, hoop). The setter changes after each round. *The group that scores the most shots within a certain number of attempts wins.*

Organizational recommendation:
Gradually increasing the distance, while simultaneously decreasing the size of the targets, will improve accuracy.

9 Setting 2-and-1

Three players stand in a triangle. A throws the ball to B; B sets the ball to C; C catches the ball and throws it back to B, etc. The passing angle should initially be quite narrow (fig. 32). After one/two errors (not catching the ball) or five successful passes in a row by one player, the players switch tasks. *The group of three that successfully completes the most passes in a row within a certain number of attempts (15, 18 etc.), wins.*

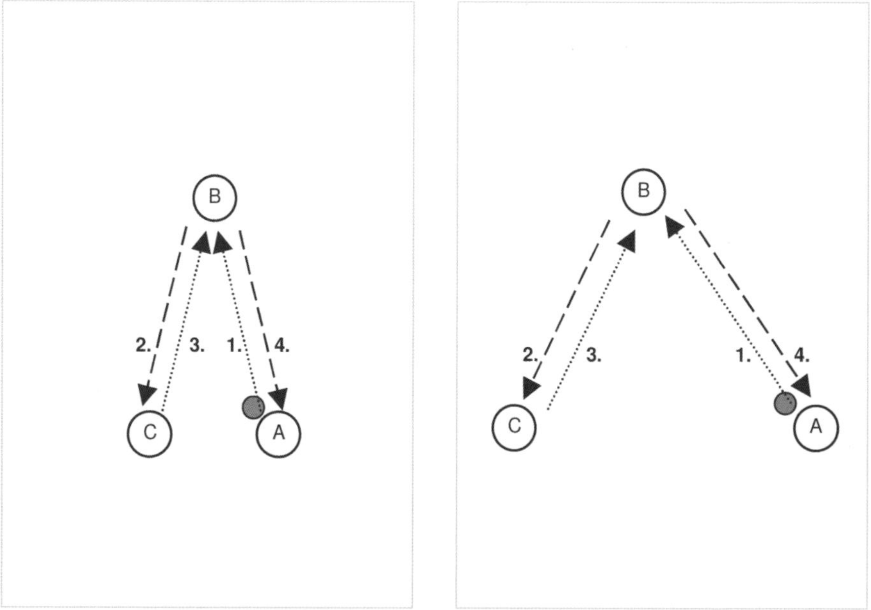

Fig. 32/33: Setting 2-and-1

Recommended actions:

- Turn in the passing direction ***before*** you touch the ball!
- Always keep an eye on your receiving and passing partner!

Variations:

1. Gradually widen the passing angle (fig. 33).
2. Two players stand on one half of the field. One of them throws the ball in the air to the other player (fig. 34) about 2 m from, and parallel to, the net from pos. IV. This player sets the ball over the net on target to the third player, who then catches the ball and passes it to the setter on the other side of the net.

Recommended actions:

- Always move at least 2 m away from the net after setting a ball.
- Remember that as a ***thrower***, you must throw your pass at least 1 m from and parallel to the net.

3. Like (1), but the ball is thrown to pos. II (fig. 35).

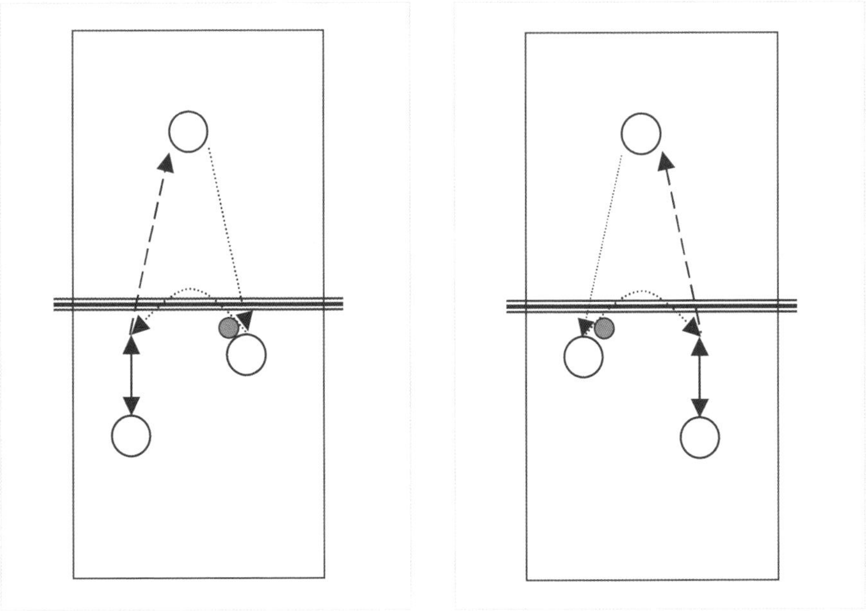

Fig. 34/35: Setting 2-and-1 over the net

10 3-and-3 play

Two teams of three face each other in an open triangle (photo 41). Every other ball must be set, meaning players take turns setting the ball within the group of six. Every volley starts with a ball that is thrown on target over the net to the other player. There are three mandatory touches on each side of the field. When an error is made (ball touches the floor, goes in the net) the players rotate, switching their right to serve. *Which group of six is able to play the longest volley over the net without errors, within a predetermined amount of time?*

Photo 41: 3-and-3 play in an open triangle

Recommended actions:

- Stick to the specified ball and running paths.
- Always set or throw the first pass diagonally, high, and at least 1 m from the net.
- Always set or throw the second pass high and parallel to the net. In your own half, always set or throw the ball to the player closest to the net.
- Play the ball over the net to different players.
- Loudly call out the name of the player you want to pass to.

Variations:

1. Players rotate by one position each time the ball crosses the net.
2. The game is played in a closed triangle formation (photo 42). The player at the net stands in the middle in pos. III and ideally plays every other touch.
3. Like (2), but with the player at the net in pos. II (photo 43).

Photos 42/43: 3-and-3 play in a closed triangle

11 2-and-2 play

Two teams of two face each other on a small field. Every second ball must be set, meaning the ball is alternately tossed in the air or set. Every volley starts with a ball that is thrown over the net on target to another player. When an error is made, the players on one side of the field switch positions and the right to serve changes over. There are three mandatory touches on each side of the field. *Which group of four will manage to play the longest volley, without errors, in a predetermined amount of time?*

Recommended actions:

- Defend one half of your field!
- Always communicate with your partner!
- When setting the ball over the net, don't always play it to the same player!
- **Remember: When a ball is played higher, it is easier to catch/set, even if it isn't very accurate!**

Variation:

4. Each time the ball crosses the net, the players on one side switch positions.

12 3-on-3 play

Game 10 "3-on-3 play" and its variations are competitive play. The initial field size is 4 x 8 m, later 4.5 x 9 m. However, every volley must begin with an overhand pass over the net by the winner of the previous volley (ball is set into the game as a serve). Player rotation takes place when their own team gets the right to serve. There are three mandatory touches. The ball that the opponent sets, or throws over the net, can always be caught. Additional errors are: ball goes off the court, into the net, touches the floor, meaning that they do not catch the ball. The game is played according to the rally point system up to 11, 15, or 25 points.

Recommended actions:

- Set the ball high and accurately to your partner!
- **Play the ball low over the net between your opponents!**

13 2-on-2 play

The rules of the game are the same as game 12 "3-on-3 play", but with two touches on each half of the field.

Variation:

With three touches, whereby every ball set/thrown over the net can be caught.

Third learning unit: Setting the ball back and forth (volley) with each other

14 1-and-1 play

The ball is set back and forth over the net in a high curve by the players facing each other on the field. *The pair with the most uninterrupted touches/most net crossings (5x, 10x, etc.), or with the fewest mistakes during a certain amount of time (two, three, etc. minutes) wins.*

Recommended actions:

- Stop before playing the ball.
- Touch the ball as briefly as possible.
- Use only the upper part of your fingers to play the ball.
- Maintain tension in your fingers.
- Playing with ten fingers is more accurate.
- The higher you set the ball, the easier it is for your teammate to get to it.
- Keep a constant eye on your teammate's positions and movements.

Variations: passing or playing?

1. 1-and-1 play with additional tasks:
   a) After passing, perform an arm circle (first forward, later backwards).
   b) After passing, touch the floor with both hands.
   c) After passing, touch your heels.
   d) After passing, touch the attack line.
   e) After passing, spin around one time, etc.
2. 1-and-1 play with four players, meaning two players stand one in front of the other on both sides of the net. After playing the ball, the player goes behind his teammate, who will play the next ball. If there is a shortage of fields/balls, play the game with three players on each side of the field.
3. Relay competition with four or more players chasing their own ball (fig. 36).

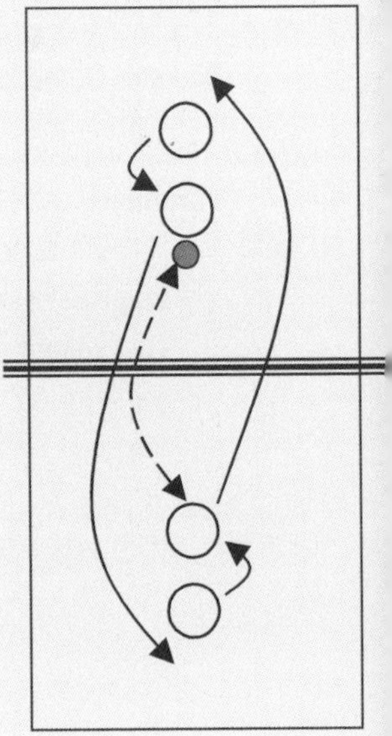

Fig. 36: Setting 1-and-1 as a relay competition

15 1-and-5 play

Five payers stand in a circle and one player stands in the middle. The player in the middle sets the ball to one of the outside players. That player passes it back with an overhand pass. The player in the middle then sets the ball to the next outside player. After two complete rounds (meaning 10 touches by the player in the middle), the players switch.

Organizational recommendation:

5-and-1 play is only recommended if there is a small number of balls.

Variations:

1. Play 1-and-4 in a square.
2. Play 1-and-3 in a triangle.

16 Setting in a triangle

Three players stand in a triangle (see fig. 32/33). Player A sets the ball to player B, B to C, C back to B, etc. (passing order: A-B-C-B-A). The passing angle should be very narrow. After one or two minutes, the players switch tasks. *The group of three that completes the most passes in a row within a certain amount of time, without errors, wins.*

Recommended action:

- Turn in the new passing direction before setting the ball!

Variations:

1. Widen the passing angle.
2. Play in a triangle formation with the passing order A-B-C-A-B-C.
3. Like variation (2), but with four or more players as well as chasing their own pass (fig. 37).
4. Play in a square with four players.
5. Setting the ball in a square, but with five or more players with chasing after their own ball (fig. 38).

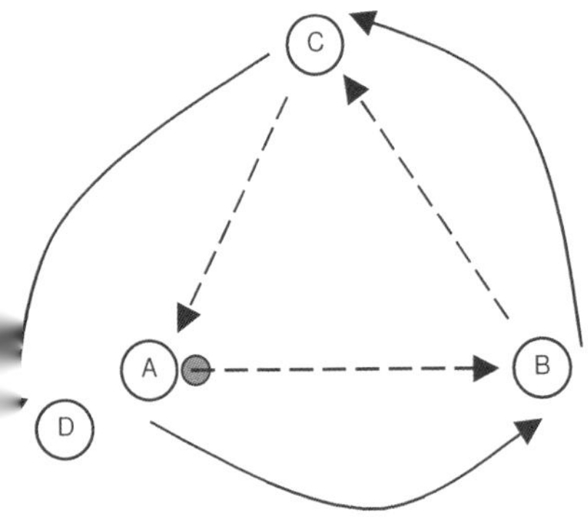

Fig. 37: Setting in a triangle with chasing the ball

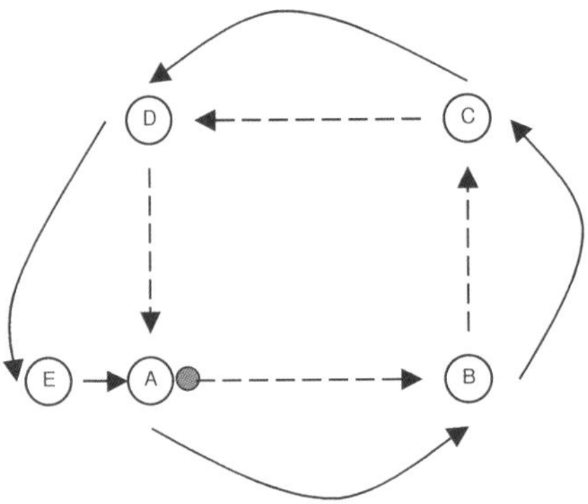

Fig. 38: Setting in a square with chasing the ball

17 3-and-3 play

Two teams of three face each other in an open triangle on two small fields (approx. 4.5 x 4.5 m). Each side has three mandatory touches (see photo series 44). During these three touches, the ball can be caught 1x on each side of the net and then played on (self-set ball). After an error, both groups rotate by one position. Which group of six can complete the longest rally over the net without errors, within a specific amount of time?

Recommended actions:

- Avoid consequential errors by setting the ball to your partner high and away from the net.
- Set the ball high and on target to one of your teammates on the opposite side.

Photo series 44

Variations:

1. Variation (1) a-f of game 14 "1-and-1 play".
2. After passing the ball over the net, a rotation takes place in the player's own group.
3. Position-based in a closed triangle with attack build-up via ***pos. III. Here variations (1) and (2) must also be taken into consideration***.
4. Position-based in a closed triangle with attack build-up via ***pos. II. Here variations (1) and (2) must also be taken into consideration***.

18 2-and-2 play

Like game 14 "1-and-1 play" and its variation (1) a-f, but initially with at least two, and later with three touches.

Recommended action:

- Communicate loudly and early with your partner, particularly for balls in the overlapping area!

Variation:

1. The game "2-and-2" and variations a-f, including a rotation within their own group after passing the ball over the net.

Fourth learning unit: Setting the ball back and forth (volley) against each other

19 1-on-1 play

Two players face each other, separated by a net, on a 2 x 4 m field and play against each other. The ball can be caught (if it can no longer be set at head level). The ball must then be set over the net from where it was caught. Errors are balls that are "out", in the net, or touching the floor. *Each player can play the ball only 1x. Players will play up to 15 or 25 points, or for time.*

Recommended actions:

- Try to read your opponent's behavior as early as possible.
- Play the ball to the back when your opponent is positioned in the front, and vice versa.
- When the opponent is in possession, quickly move to the center of the field to be in an ideal starting position.
- Avoid easy mistakes.

Variations:

1. "1-on-1" play with additional tasks:
   a) Perform an arm circle with both arms after passing the ball.
   b) Touch the floor with both hands after passing the ball.
   c) Touch your heels after passing the ball.
   d) Touch the attack line after passing the ball.
   e) Touch the centerline after passing the ball.
   f) Spin around one time after passing the ball.
2. Vary the field size: Choose a field that is 3 x 4 m, 2 x 6 m, or 3 x 6 m. **Variations (1) a-f apply to each field size.**
3. Variations (1) and (2) on different fields with a "moat" as open space (fig. 39).

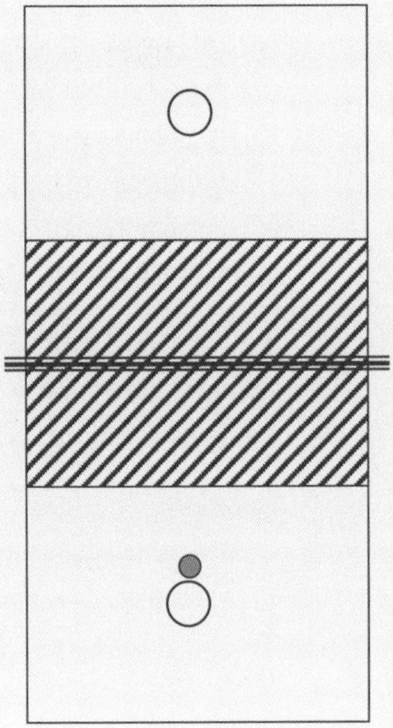

Fig. 39: Setting 1-on-1 across a moat

4. Variations (1) to (3), but a point counts double when a player scores it without first catching the ball. All points scored after catching the ball continue to be single points.

Organizational recommendation:
For motivational reasons, all competitive games (1-on-1, 3-on-3, etc.) and their variations should be played as a setting competition based on the "Emperor's ball tournament mode" (see fig. 11).

20 3-on-3 play

Playing concept, rules, and competitive modes as in game 19 "1-on-1 play", but initially with at least two touches. Only the ball set over the net by the opponent can be caught without counting as an error. The field size is 4 x 8 m. The teams of three play in an open triangle formation. A player from the team that scores a point sets the ball into the game from behind the attack line.

Variations:

1. This game with three touches.
2. Field size is 4.5 x 9 m.
3. This game with additional tasks (see game 19 "1-on-1", variation (1) a-f).
4. Players rotate within their group after playing a pass.
5. Position-based in closed triangle formation with attack build-up via ***pos. III. Variations (1) – (4) also apply here.***
6. Position-based in closed triangle formation with attack build-up via ***pos. II. Variations (1) – (4) also apply here.***

21 2-on-2 play

Like game 19 ("1-on-1 play") and game 20 ("3-on-3 play) and their variations on a 3 x 6 m field. A minimum of two mandatory touches applies.

Variations:

1. This game with three touches.
2. Field size is 4 x 8 m.

2.2 BUMP (FOREARM PASS)

The three most important movement characteristics are:

- Body-ball relationship: ***"Player is behind the ball"*** (photo 45).
- Target area: ***"Play the ball with the forearms and arms extended and hands interlocked"*** (photo 46).
- Initiation (for passers): ***"Straighten the legs and use shoulder momentum"*** (photo 47). When the ball has to travel farther to the receiver, the momentum only comes from the shoulders if possible, and with faster approaching balls, the ball is received by pulling the arms back to the body (defensive bump).

Photo 45

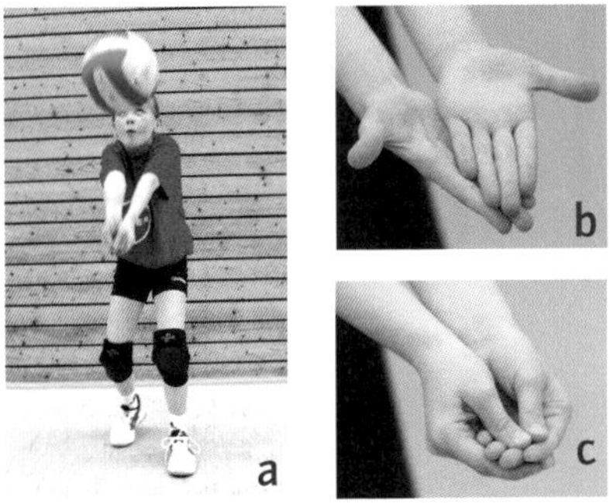

Photo 46

Photo 47

Photo series 48: Movement sequence for the bump

First learning unit: Bumping a ball thrown by another player

This learning unit is largely similar to the ***second learning unit for the "overhand pass"***.

1 1-and-1 play

The ball is thrown to the opposite player in a high arc (over the net) so that he can receive it at hip level. The player bumps it back so that his teammate can set and then catch it. Players switch after five bumps. *The pair that bumps the ball 5x, 10x, etc. in a row without the ball touching the floor and the ball is always set/caught by the partner, wins.*

If you have access to a volleyball court, the starting player should stand in the attack zone, and throw the ball from there over the net, into the opposing attack zone (fig. 40). The partner, on the other side of the net, stands in his starting position behind the attack zone and only moves into the attack zone to play the ball. He must leave the attack zone before the next underhand touch. This ensures that the bumping player is always positioned behind the ball. The ball's high trajectory, resulting from the high net and short distances between players, forces players to play the ball with their bodies and particularly with their legs extended.

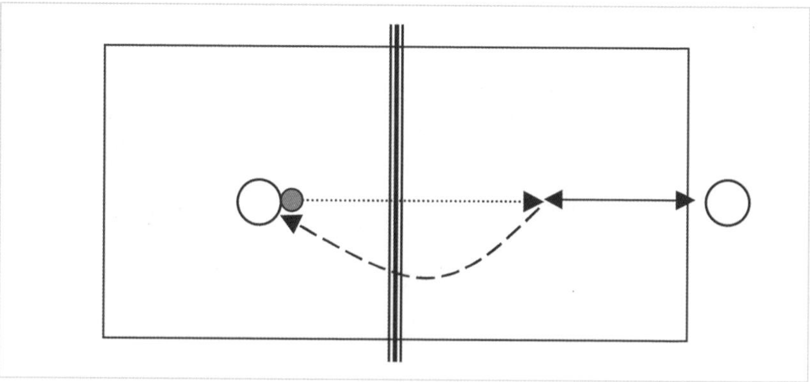

Fig. 40: Bumping 1-and-1 after moving

Recommended actions:

- Throw the ball accurately ***in front*** of your partner.
- Move quickly to the ball.
- Stand behind the ball in passing direction (but in a safe position).
- Hold your extended arms nearly parallel to your thighs.
- Extend your body towards the ball.

Variations:

1. Gradually increase the distances between the players and between the players and the net.
2. 1-and-3 play: The single player alternately throws the ball to one of the three other players who initially stand one behind the other, and later, next to each other (see fig. 30/31). That player then bumps the ball back to him. If the single player is unable to set the ball, the two players trade places.
3. The ball is bumped back into the opposing field on a target (mat, hoop, etc.). The group that scores the most points during a specified number of attempts wins. The thrower changes after every round.

Methodical recommendation:

The exercise/game ***"Bumping the ball up"*** is recommended if students already struggle with the easy version of the game.

This can be done in two steps:

a) Let the low self-set ball bounce on the floor, then bump it up and subsequently catch it.

b) Using your legs for support, bump the ball as many times in a row as possible. The arms should be parallel to the floor (overcorrection) (photo 49). Game: *Who can bump the ball the most times in a row without an error, within a certain amount of time?*

Photo 49: Arm position for the bump

2 Bumping 2-and-1

Three players stand in a triangle. Player A throws the ball to B, B bumps it to C, C sets the ball, catches it, and throws it back to B, etc. (see fig. 32/33). The initial passing angle should be acute. After a player makes one/two error(s) (not catching the ball), or five successful bumps in a row, the players switch tasks. *The group of three that completes the most bumps in a row without making an error within a certain number of attempts, wins.*

Recommended actions:

- Turn before you touch the ball.
- Always keep your eyes on the target.
- It is better to play the ball high than low.

Variations:

1. Two players stand on one side of the field. Player A throws a low ball in front of his teammate B, parallel to the net approximately 2 m from pos. IV. B bumps the ball accurately over the net to the third player C, who then sets the ball, catches it, and passes it to A on the other side of the net (see fig. 34).
2. Like (1), but the ball is thrown to pos. II (see fig. 35).

Recommended action:

- As the ***thrower***, remember to throw your pass at least 1 m in front of and parallel to the net!

3 3-and-3 play

Two teams of three face each other in an ***open triangle***. Players must bump every other ball, meaning the ball is alternately thrown or bumped (photo 50). Every volley starts with a low ball thrown over the net and right in front of the teammate. There are three mandatory touches per side. When an error is made (ball touches the floor, goes in the net), the players rotate and the right to serve or throw the ball changes. *Which group of six can complete the longest series of net crossings, without any mistakes within a certain amount of time?*

Variations:

1. Players rotate one position every time the ball crosses the net.
2. The game is played in a closed triangle formation. The player at the net stands in the middle in pos. III and should play every other touch.
3. Like (2), but the player at the net is in pos. II (photo 51).

) 50: Bumping in an open triangle

Photo 51: Bumping with the setter in pos. II

4 2-and-2 play

The ball passed by player A via a throw in their own half is bumped over the net by his partner B. Teammate C on the opposite side sets it high, catches it and throws it to his partner D on their side of the field, etc. (fig. 41). Two touches are mandatory. *Which group of four can complete the longest series of net-crossings without making any mistakes, within a certain amount of time?*

Recommended actions:

- Bump the ball high and diagonally away from the net.
- Alternately bump the ball to the players on the opposite side.

Variation:

1. Each time the ball crosses the net, players on one side of the net switch positions.

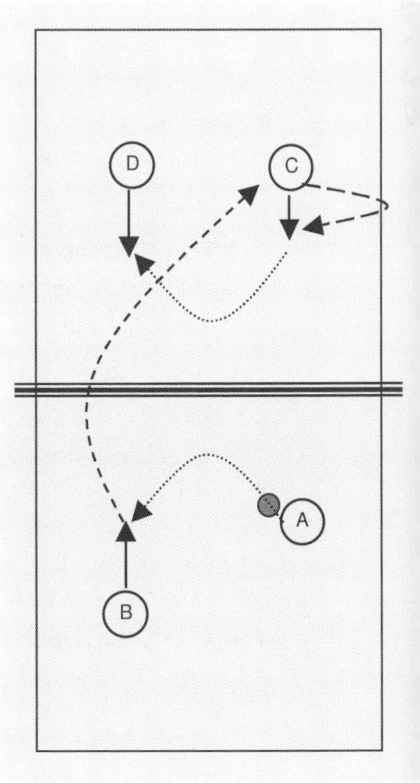

Fig. 41: 2-and-2 play

5 3-on-3 play

Game 3 "3-on-3 play" and its variations are competitive. The field size is 4 x 8 m. However, every volley has to start with an overhand pass over the net by the winner of the previous volley (ball is set into the game as a serve). Players rotate whenever their own team gets the right to serve. Three touches are mandatory. Every ball the opponent plays over the net can be caught. Rules of the game apply. *Game is scored via the rally point system up to 11, 15, or 25 points.*

Variations:

1. The ball can no longer be caught.
2. Field size is 4.5 x 9 m.

6 2-on-2 play

The same rules as game 5 "3-on-3 play" and their variations 1) and 2) apply, but with at least two touches on each side of the field.

Variation:

1. Three mandatory touches.

Second learning unit: Bumping the ball set by another player

In this learning unit, all of the various bumping versions introduced in the previous first learning unit can be played instead of throwing or setting the ball. For reasons listed in the theoretical part of the book, it is important that the children do not play doubles, meaning the ball is set to the partner and not thrown. The ball that is bumped to the partner is first received by setting and then caught, and subsequently played overhand to the partner.

Organizational advice:
All of the games are easy to implement when the ball set by the partner is played high, but arrives in front of the teammate so he/she is behind the ball when making contact with it.

Third learning unit: Setting and bumping volleys as a team

In this learning unit, all of the "setting" games introduced in the third learning unit can be played by using the two passing techniques, setting and bumping. The ball can NO LONGER be caught!

Recommended actions:

- Move quickly so you can set as many balls as possible.
- Only bump balls that you are unable to set.
- You must bump very shallow and fast-approaching balls.
- Remember that it is easier for your partner to reach a ball that has been thrown higher.
- It is better to play the ball high and less accurate than shallow and on target.
- It is better to play the ball from farther away than too close to the net.
- Always communicate with all of your teammates (photos 52-54).

Photo 54: Poor communication

Photos 52/53: Good communication

Fourth learning unit: Setting and bumping volleys against each other

In this learning unit, all of the "setting" games introduced in the fourth learning unit can now also be played with both setting techniques.

Recommended actions:

- Keep an eye on your opponent so you can immediately recognize where he intends to play the ball!
- **Always choose your starting position so you have approximately two-thirds of your side of the court in front of you (photo 55). Remember: It is easier to get to the ball when moving forward instead of backwards!**
- Vary your attacking behavior by changing the direction and length of your passes.
- Watch your opponent so you can place the ball between the opposing players, or play the ball into lightly covered zones.
- The player that calls it first or first moves towards the ball plays it.

Photo 55: Starting position when receiving and defending

Methodical recommendations:
Overhand play with a jump should be learned as a TWO-HANDED FEINT ATTACK no later than when playing against opponents, while learning the two passing techniques, but before introducing the shot/spin spike (photo series 56). Here it is advisable to hold individual competitions, as well as, all game variations and games with and against each other with the jump pass as an attacking action. *The introduction of the two-handed feint attack is like that of the spin spike (see chapter 2.3).*

At this point, the "timing games" (see chapter 1.2 "General preparatory games with a ball", games 27 or 29) must have been practiced intensively and must have been mastered. They represent the most important requirement for every jumping action in volleyball.

Photo series 56: Movement sequence setting the ball from a jump (two-handed feint attack)

2.3 SHOT/SPIN SPIKE (AND FEINT ATTACK/TIP)

After introducing the two-handed feint attack in the previous chapter, the shot/spin spike should be introduced, for motivational reasons, as the first ***real*** attacking action. ***In addition, the two-handed (and single-handed) feint attack/tip should continue to be used as an alternative action during the following learning unit on the shot/spin spike.*** This is easier to implement and can better offset a bad pass, meaning that the feint attack is important to avoid one's own mistakes.

The introduction and development of the shot/spin spike is identical to the method of the two-handed and single-handed jump-feint/tip attack over the net. But hereinafter, we will only introduce the new basic technique for the shot/spin spike. All games and game variations also apply to the two-handed and single-handed jump-feint attack/tip over the net.

The three most important movement characteristics of the shot/spin spike include:

- Playing stance: ***"After taking an explosive forward step to push off (photo series 60) jump up with both legs UNDER the ball"*** (photo 57).
- Contact area and timing: ***"Hit the ball with the palm of the hand AT THE HIGHEST POINT of the jump"*** (photo 58).
- Creating momentum: ***"Hit the ball in a curve from below and behind, into the back of the court by extending the arm and using the wrist"*** (photo 59).

Photo 57

Photo 58

Photo 59

Photo series 60: Movement sequence shot/spin spike

First learning unit: Throwing the ball up and attacking it

1 Hitting a target from a standing position

The player stands 2-3 feet from a wall that has a mark (line) drawn on it at a height of about 2 m. He throws the ball underhand with both hands above head-level, and then hits it against the wall above the mark with one hand. *The player that hits the target the most during a certain number of attempts (10, 15, 20 balls) wins.*

Recommended actions:

- Don't throw the ball higher than 1 m above head-level.
- Stand under the ball when you hit it.
- Bend the hitting arm when you gather momentum as though you were trying to stick your hand in your "backpack" (photo 61).
- Extend the hitting arm when you make contact with the ball as though you were pulling your hand out of your "backpack" (photo 62).
- Hit the ball with an open palm (photo 62).
- Make sure your hit is carefully targeted instead of hard.

Photos 61 / 62: Shot/spin spike from a standing position

Variations:

1. The ball that bounces off the wall after the attack should be caught.
2. The ball that bounces off the wall after the attack should be set overhead and then caught.
3. Players stand on the attack line of the mini volleyball court and hit the ball into the opposite side of the court.
4. The ball must be hit into the half of the court behind the attack line.
5. The ball must be hit into the left or right side of the court.
6. The ball must be hit 3 x into each the left and right side of the court.
7. The ball must hit specific targets (mats, vaulting boxes, hoops).

2 1-and-1 play with shot/spin spike from a standing position

Two players stand on opposite sides of the net. The ball is hit to the partner, who catches it (one point), or a player sets the ball for himself overhand or underhand and then catches it (two points). He then hits the ball back to his partner. *Which team of two will be first to complete a sequence of five, seven, nine actions (five, seven, nine points) in a row without any mistakes?*

3 Hitting a target from a jump

Like game 1 "Hitting a target from a standing position" and its variations (3) to (7), only the ball is attacked from a jump.

Recommended actions:

- In case of timing problems: First repeat general timing exercises ***(see chapter 1.2 "General preparatory games with a ball", games 27 and 29)*** and subsequently overhand passing from a jump.
- As you jump, move both arms from back to front and up to gather momentum for your jump.
- Engage your wrist when hitting the ball from below/back so it has a curved trajectory.
- Use the two-handed jump pass in response to imprecise serves.

4 1-and-1 play with shot/spin spike hit from a jump

Like game 2 "1-and-1 play with shot/spin spike from a standing position", only the ball is hit/set from a jump.

5 1-on-1 play with shot/spin spike from a standing position

Like game 2 "1-and-1 play with shot/spin spike from a standing position", but against each other on a 3 x 8 m court. The ball cannot be hit into the first 1.5 m behind the net. Only balls that go off the court or touch the floor, meaning balls that are not caught, are considered errors. *The rally point system is used for scoring up to 15 or 25 points.*

Variation:

1. Court size is 3 x 10 m to start, then changes to 2 x 8 m, and finally 2 x 10 m.

6 1-on-1 play with shot/spin spike from a jump

Like game 5 "1-on-1 play with shot/spin spike from a standing position" and its variations, only the ball is attacked from a jump.

Second learning unit: Attacking a ball thrown by another player

7 Safety attack

The ball must be hit from pos. IV into the opposite side of the court preferably from a jump. Each group consists of three attackers and one setter who will set the ball approximately 1.5 m higher than the net (fig. 42). *The group that hits the most balls into the opposing court, within a certain amount of time (three or five minutes), wins. Balls attacked from a jump count lead to double points.* The server changes after each round.

Recommended actions:

- Throw the ball into the air evenly with both hands and farther away from the net (instead of too close).
- Watch the flying height of the thrown ball.
- Jump like you plan to catch the ball at its highest point.
- Forcefully swing your arms forward and up from behind/below.
- Jump vertically, meaning you take off from, and land, in the same spot.
- Jump using both legs.

Variations:

1. The server's distance is increased to 2.5 m.
2. The shot/spin spike comes from pos. II.

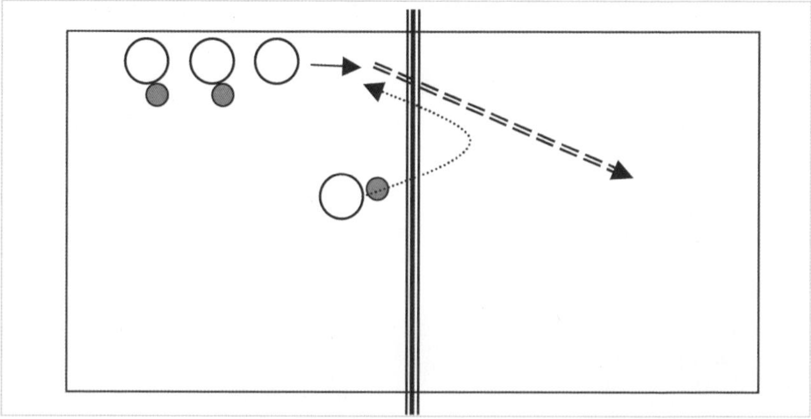

Fig. 42: Shot/spin spike after the serve/set

8 Hitting a target from a standing position or from a jump

Like game 7 "Safety attack" with all its variations, but the ball must be hit into the right or left side of the court.

Variations:

1. The ball must be hit 3 x into each the right and left side of the court.
2. The ball must hit specific, increasingly smaller targets (mats, vaulting boxes, hoops).
3. The ball must be hit into the right or left side of the court according to the server's verbal command.

9 3-and-3 play (Canadian volley)

Canadian volley means that every other touch in their own court must be done by catching/throwing the ball, meaning the passing action is always either a serve or a pass, in order to promote flow of play.

Three players stand on each side of the net in an open triangle formation. The back-row player brings the ball into the game by setting it diagonally to the teammate in direction of pos. II. This player catches the ball and then throws it on target, as parallel to the net as possible, to the third player in pos. IV (without moving with the ball). The third player will then perform a shot/spin spike if possible from a jump (or a standing position or overhand pass from a jump, etc.) over the net to the three players on the other side. One of the three, receives the ball by setting or bumping it, and plays it appropriately high and diagonally towards the net. The player in this zone runs to the net, catches the ball and then sets it parallel to the net in order for his front player to attack. Rotations are done by time or after three or five errors.
Which group of six will manage to play the most net crossings within a certain amount of time without an error?

Variations:

1. Net crossings are only those actions played with a shot/spin spike or a two-handed feint attack from a jump.
2. Like variation (1), but only the shot/spin spike from a jump counts as a successful net crossing.

3. Both variations in terms of position-based attack build-up via pos. III, later via pos. II.
4. Players rotate by one position after playing the ball over the net.

10 2-and-2 play (Canadian volley)

Like game 9 "3-and-3 play (Canadian volley)" and its variations (1), (2), and (4).

11 3-on-3 play (Canadian volley)

Like game 9 "3-and-3 play (Canadian volley)" with all its variations, but played against each other on a 4.5 x 10 m court. Only out-of-bounds balls and balls that touch the floor, or not catching the second ball, count as errors. *The rally point system is used to score the game up to 15 or 25 points.*

Variation:

1. Court measurements are 4.5 x 12 m, later 4.5 x 14 m.

12 2-on-2 play (Canadian volley)

Like game 11 "3-on-3 play (Canadian volley)" with its variations, but played with teams of two.

All Canadian volley games can/should be played in the "Emperor's ball tournament mode"!

Third learning unit: Attacking a ball set by another player

During this learning unit, all of the shot/spin spike games previously introduced in the second learning unit should be played again. The only difference is that the passing player catches the ball, tosses it to himself, and then ***sets it for the attacker*** as a passing action (expanded Canadian volley).

Fourth learning unit: Playing volleys with each other

13 3-and-3 play

Like game 9 "3-and-3 (Canadian volley)" in the second learning unit on the shot/spin spike with all its variations, only ***the ball can no longer be caught*** but must always be played on as a ***volley***. Instead of a serve, the ball is set from their own attack zone to behind the opposing attack line.

14 2-and-2 play

Like game 13 "3-and-3 play" with variations, but played in teams of two.

Fifth learning unit: Playing volleys against each other

During this learning unit players should play all of the shot/spin spike game variations, introduced in the previous fourth learning unit, against each other. ***Possible variations*** include scoring, which means that a successful undefended (meaning no second touch is possible) shot/spin spike from a jump scores three points (photo 63), a successful shot/spin spike from a standing position, or a two-handed overhand pass from a jump scores two points, etc.

Methodical recommendations:
During all competitive games the approaching ball from the opponent can INITIALLY be caught to promote defensive actions and flow of play!

If frequent game interruptions occur, the Canadian volley games should be played again intensively!

Photo 63: Shot/spin spike in 3-on-3 play

2.4 UNDERHAND SERVE

The three most important movement characteristics are:

- Creating momentum: ***"Pendular arm movement with extended arm parallel to the body with leg extension"*** (photo 64).
- Body-to-ball relationship: ***"Hit the shallowly served ball (15 cm max.) from behind/below"*** (photo 65).
- Target area: ***"Hit the ball with an open and firm palm"*** (photo 66).

Photo 64

Photo 65

Photo 66

Photo series 67: Movement sequence underhand serve

First learning unit: Serving to a target/partner

1 Targeted serve against a wall

Players serve the ball underhand against a wall from a distance of 3 m. The ball should hit the wall above a mark/line at a height of approximately 3 m. *The player or group (consisting of 2-5 players) that is first to complete 5, 10, 15 successful actions, wins.*

Recommended actions:

- First gather momentum with your hitting arm and then do a very shallow serve with one hand.
- Serve the ball in extension of the hitting arm.

Variations:

1. Successful actions must occur consecutively.
2. Like the game and variation (1), but by gradually increasing the distance to the wall to 6 m.

2 Targeted serve over the net

Players serve the ball underhand from the attack line into the opposing court. *Which player is the first to complete 5, 10, 15 underhand serves over the net (error-free and consecutively)?*

Variations:

1. Like the game, but the distance to the net gradually increases to 5 or 7 m.

Recommended action:

- Position yourself in the center of the baseline behind your side of the court.

2. Like the game and the variation, but players must alternate hitting into the left and the right side of the court.
3. The served ball should hit targets (mats, vaulting boxes, etc.). First one target, then the other, and finally alternating between them.

Second learning unit: Serving to a partner

3 1-and-1 serving game

Two partners are positioned on either side of the net. The serving player stands behind the baseline (court measurements 3 x 6/8 m) and his partner stands on the opposite court. He catches the serve and rolls the ball back to the server. Players switch tasks after five serves. *The pair that catches the most error-free serves wins.*

Variations:

1. Like the game, but the ball is received by setting it (or bumping) and then caught. Players alternate serving.
2. The receiving player stands on a mat/inside a hoop, etc., which he is not allowed to leave to receive the ball.

4 2-and-3 serving game

Two players take turns serving underhand to a group of three players standing in an open triangle formation. The group plays the received ball to the net in accordance with a situation-based attack build-up, where the setter catches it and rolls it back to the respective server (fig. 43). Payers rotate by one position (including one of the servers) after a total of eight serve attempts. *Which group will be the first to successfully receive the ball 25, 30, 35 times?* This game can also be played with only one server.

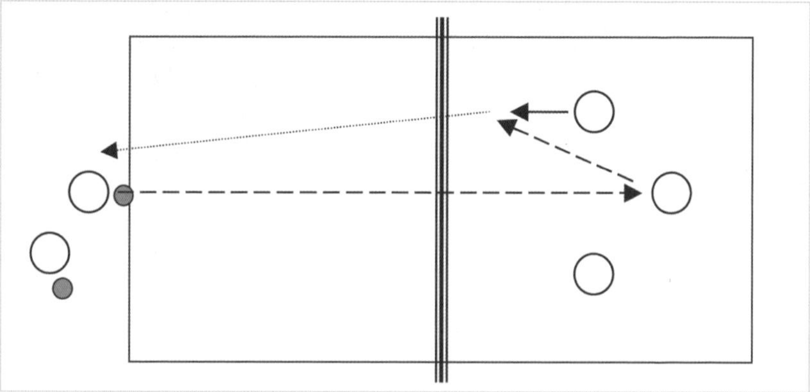

Fig. 43: 2-and-3 serving game

Variations:

1. Like the game, but the ball is not caught by the passing player but instead played to the attacker, who will catch the ball.
2. Like the game and variation (1), but in a closed triangle, meaning ***position-based*** with attack build-up via pos. III, later via pos. II.

5 2-and-2 serving game

Like game 4 "2-and-3 serving game" with variation (1), but with receiving the ball with a two-player defense.

Recommended actions:

- Deflect the ball in a high arc.
- Play the first pass at least 1 m from the net.

Third learning unit: Playing volleys with each other

6 2-and-3 serving game

Like variations (1) and (2) of game 4 "2-and-3 serving play" in the previous learning unit, only the attacker does not catch the ball but plays a targeted shot/spin spike, or a two-handed feint attack from a jump to the server who has run onto the court (fig. 44). *If the server manages to catch the ball, the group of five scores one point.*

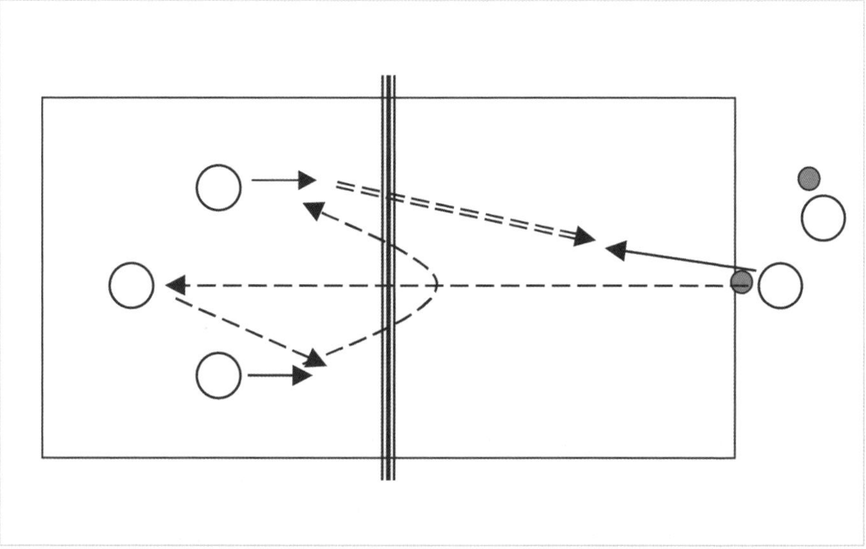

Fig. 44: Serving play with attack build-up

Variation:

1. Like the game, but the server first defends the ball and then catches it.

7 2-and-2 serving play

Like game 6 "2-and-3 serving play" and its variation, but players receive the ball with a two-player defense.

Fourth learning unit: Playing volleys against each other

8 2-on-3 serving play

The two serving players alternate hitting the ball to the three opposing players who are positioned in an open triangle on a 4.5 x 9 m court. They are supposed to use their learned skills to play the ball back over the net with at least two touches, forcing the server that has run onto the court to be unable to catch the ball. After a total of 10 serves, the group of five rotates by one position so that each player has acted as server twice after five rotations. *The player with the most serves that either are not returned, or returned in a way that allows him to catch the ball, wins.*

Recommended actions:

- Avoid making easy mistakes by using a reliable attacking technique (shot/spin spike from a standing position, overhand pass from a jump, etc.).
- It is better to play into undefended zones on the court from a standing position than from a jump to the defender.
- Serve the ball into insufficiently covered zones.
- Serve between players.
- Change the ball's trajectory and the length of the serve.
- Keep a close eye on the serving /defending player.

Variations:

1. Like the game, but the server must deflect the ball and then catch it.
2. Like the game, but the two servers act as a team and defend the court together (rotating serves and number of serves stay the same). *The team of two with the most successful actions wins.*
3. Like variation (2), but a 2-on-3 game develops, meaning the serving team tries to play the ball back into the opposing court with no more than three touches. Scoring: Rally point system, meaning both teams can score, but the servers get two points for an ace serve, or when they win a rally. The team of three receives one point for every successful rally. *The first team of two or team of three to reach 10 points wins.*
4. Like the game and variations (1) and (3), but now the team of three must perform three mandatory touches.

5. Like variation (4), but the team of three must perform their third touch from a jump.
6. Like the game and all variations, but in a closed triangle, meaning position-based with attack build-up via pos. III, later via pos. II.

9 2-on-2 serving play

Like game 8 "2-on-3 serving play" and its variations (1) and (5), but with two defenders.

10 One-sided 3-on-3 play

One team has the serving right in a 3-on-3 game in an ***open triangle formation***. After five serves, both teams rotate by one position. After 15 serves, the right to serve goes to the other team. The serving team gets one point whenever the receiving team is unable to play the ball back over the net. This also applies to multiple net crossings. The defending team gets a point when a serving error is made or when the opposing team makes an error during play. *The team that has scored the most points after 30 serves wins.*

Variations:

1. Like the game but in a closed triangle, meaning position-based with attack build-up via pos. III, later via pos. II.
2. As a one-sided 2-on-2 game.

2.5 MINI VOLLEYBALL AS A COMPETITIVE GAME

Mini volleyball refers to the application of the basic techniques and tactics learned in the present concept in a competitive game: two teams consisting of three players each face off on a mini-volleyball court (4.5 x 12 m). The net height is 2.10 m. Figures 45-47 show all of the possible basic formations during their own and the opposing serve/possession.

Fig. 45 shows the teams' formation with a situation-based attack build-up (receiving the ball in an open triangle).

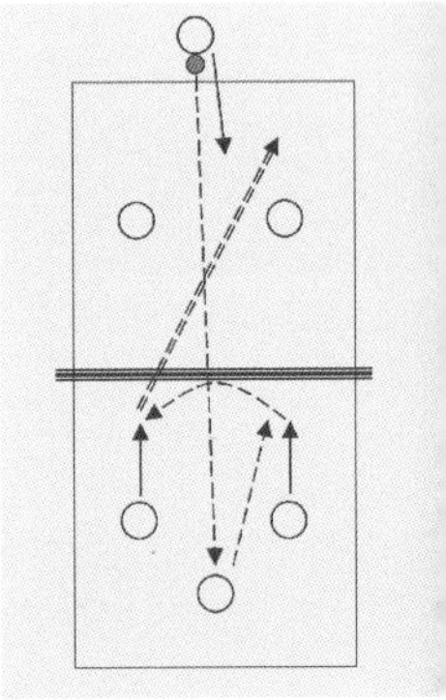

Fig. 45

Fig. 46 and photo 68 show the teams' formation for a position-based attack build-up via pos. III (receiving the ball in a closed triangle).

Fig. 46/Photo 68

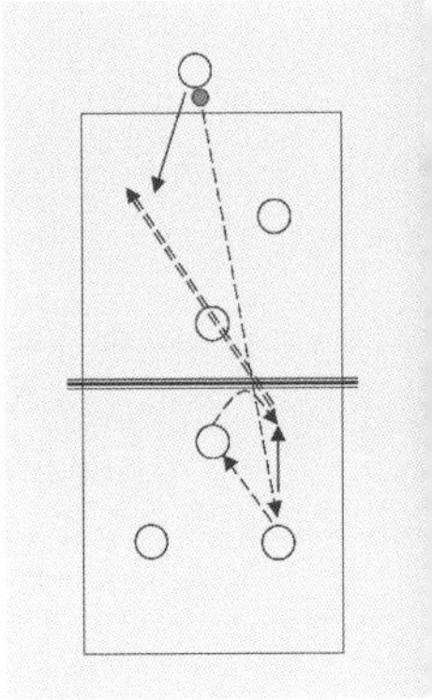

Fig. 47 and photo 69 show the teams' formation for a position-based attack build-up via pos. II (receiving the ball in a closed triangle).

Fig. 47/Photo 69

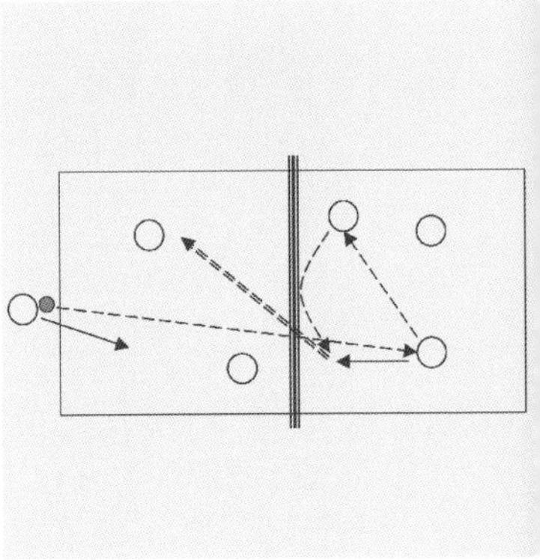

Rules

- If a player/team has two successful serves in a row, the team rotates by one position and the next player plays the next serve (Portuguese rule).
- If the ball touches the gym's ceiling after it has been received/defended (first touch), the same team can continue to play the ball.

Please note:

Exemplary youth division special rules listed here:

Age group U13 (age 12 and younger):

- For girls and boys, the net height is 2.10 m and the court dimensions are 6 x 6 m.
- Position changes are not allowed.
- Continuing to play a ball after it has touched the ceiling is unfortunately no longer permitted.
- When receiving the opposing serve, it must unfortunately be done in a closed triangle, meaning two-player defense, and passed via the middle player at the net (photo 70). Thus only a position-based attack build-up is allowed (which is inexplicable for methodological and didactical reasons!). In age group U12 (age 11 and younger), players play 2-on-2. The court measures 4.5 x 4.5 m and the net height is 2.05 m.

Photo 70: Attack build-up via pos. III

2.6 MINI VOLLEYBALL BY INTERNATIONAL RULES

Mini volleyball by international rules allows all basic techniques and their variations, meaning overhand serve, spike, as well as the block.

Mini volleyball is a standardized game, which means that the rules are internationally identical, so sanctioned tournaments are not only played nationally but also internationally (photo 71).

We ***deliberately*** chose to omit the game of mini volleyball by international rules from this tutorial because the overhand serve, the spike, as well as the block result in frequent game interruptions, can lead to shortened rallies, decreased playing intensity and joy of playing, and motivation which is counterproductive to the teaching of this game sport.

Photo 71: International mini volleyball tournament

2.7 MIDI VOLLEYBALL

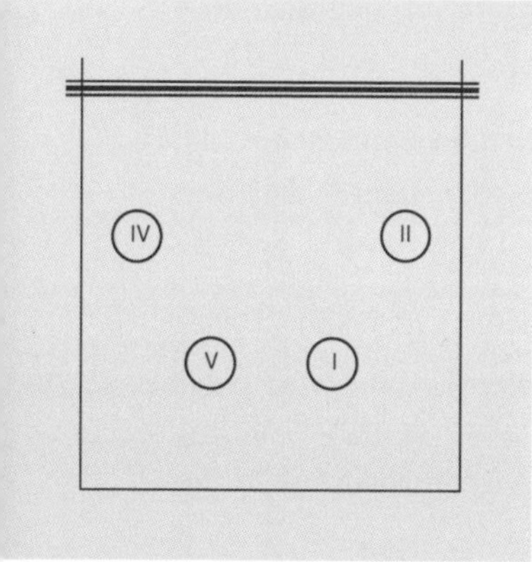

Based on mini volleyball with a three-player serve-receive formation and situation-based attack build-up, meaning playing in an open triangle, the transition to ***midi volleyball*** "4-on-4 play" on a larger court (at first 6 x 12 m, later 7 x 14 m) takes place. In this game, players begin with a ***four-player serve-receive formation in a semi-circle*** (fig. 48), ***the attack is built via the two front-row players*** who, as the two outside players, will handle the setting or rather the attack.

Fig. 48: Midi volleyball with four-player serve-receive formation (receiving in a semi-circle)

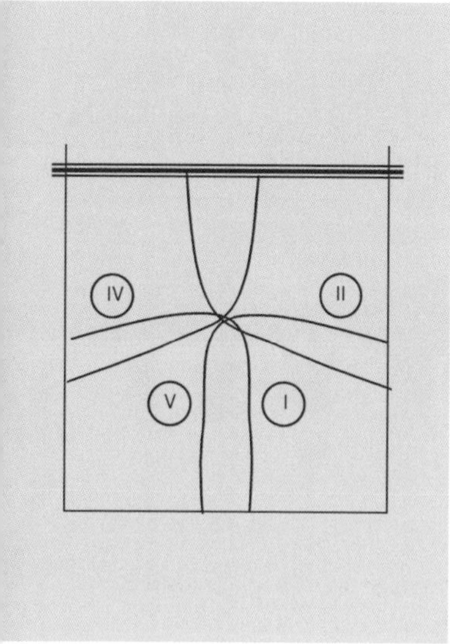

Fig. 49

Fig. 49 shows the receiving area and its seams when receiving the ball in a semi-circle.

The court is divided into two halves to facilitate better understanding of the game, and easier implementation of the situation-based attack built-up with a four-player defense.

If the opposing team's serve goes into court half A, the ball is received diagonally to the player on pos. II at the net, who will then act as setter and play to the attacker in pos. IV (fig. 50/photos 72-74). If the ball is received in the opposite location in court half B, the attack build-up takes place in mirror reverse, meaning the player in pos. IV runs to the net, acts as the setter and plays to the player in pos. II. The player at the right back of the court acts as server, i.e. the player in pos. 1 (fig. 51).

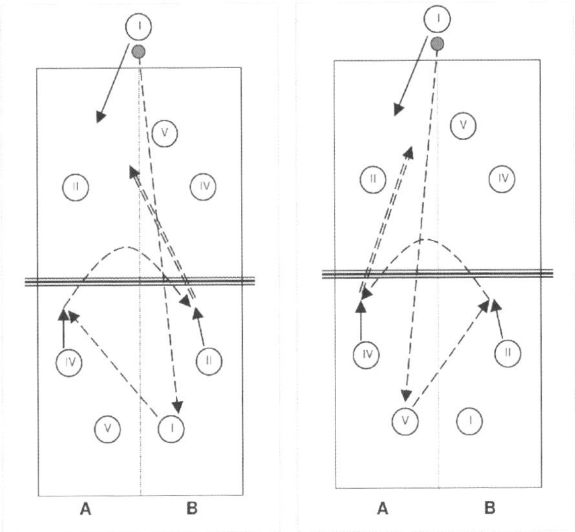

Fig. 50/51: Attack build-up with a four-player serve-receive formation (receiving in a semi-circle)

Photos 72-74: Attack build-up with a four-player serve-receive formation (receiving in a semi-circle)

The defensive formation is largely identical to the receiving formation since midi volleyball should initially also be played without spikes, and thus without the block.

A variation of the four-player serve-receive formation with situation-based attack build-up can be seen in fig. 52/53. In the ***zigzag serve-receive formation***, the front-row players are in pos. IV and III and back-row players are in pos. VI and I.

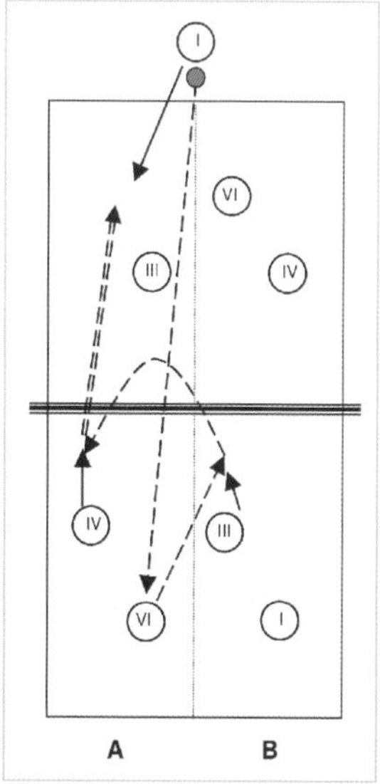

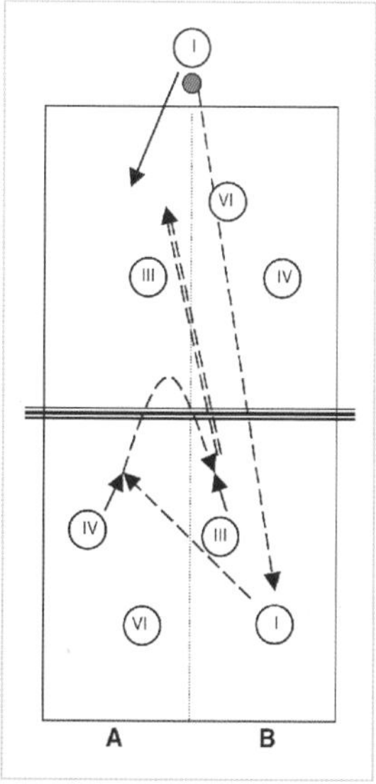

Fig. 52/53:
Attack build-up with a four-player serve-receive formation (zigzag serve-receive formation)

Fig. 54 shows the receiving areas and their seams in the zigzag formation.

If players IV and VI receive the ball on court-half A, player III handles the set (photos 75-78). If the ball is received in court-half B, the front-row player IV handles the setting.

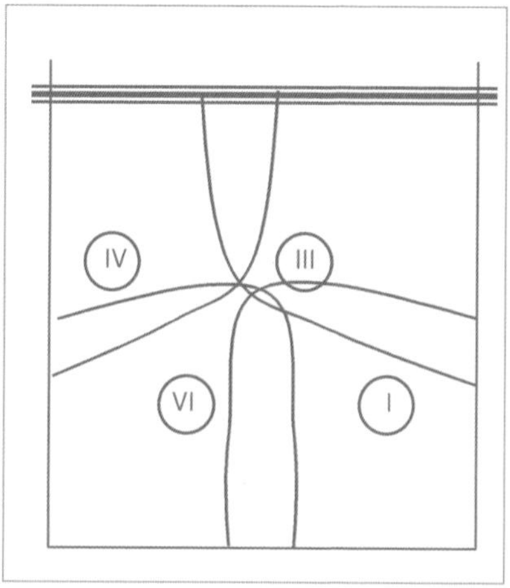

Fig. 54

Photos 75-78: Attack build-up with a four-player serve-receive formation (zigzag serve-receive formation)

The following two figures 55/56 show the zigzag serve-receive formation with players III and II as front-row players and VI/I and V as back-row players.

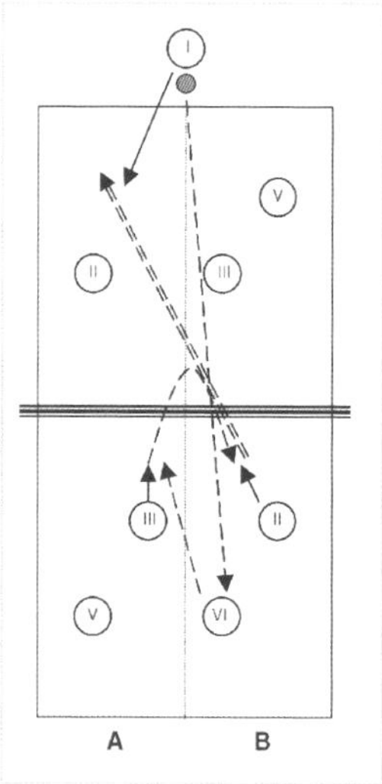

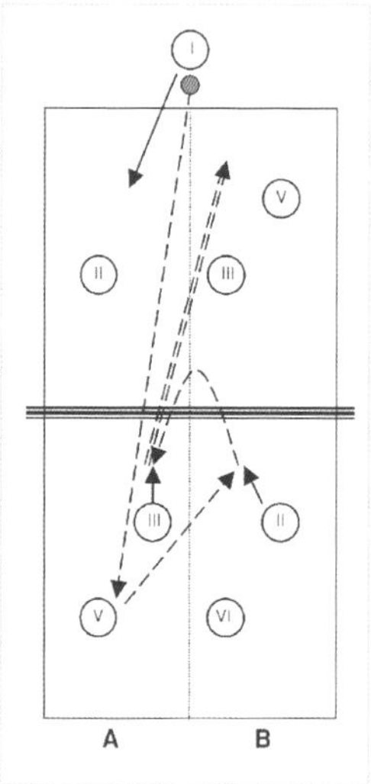

Fig. 55/56

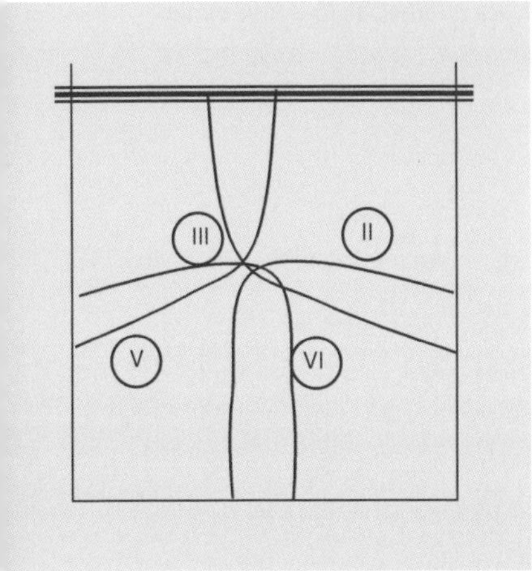

Fig. 57 shows the respective seam areas. Both versions of the zigzag serve-receive formation can also be played without back-row players, meaning all four players can be used as attackers.

The zigzag formations are a good choice because on the one hand they provide good coverage of the center of the court, and on the other hand the receiving and passing distances are shorter than with a four-player semi-circle/U formation.

Fig. 57

For a ***position-based attack build-up*** via pos. III (fig. 58/photo 79), the team consists of three front-row players (pos. II, III, IV) and one back-row player (pos. VI).

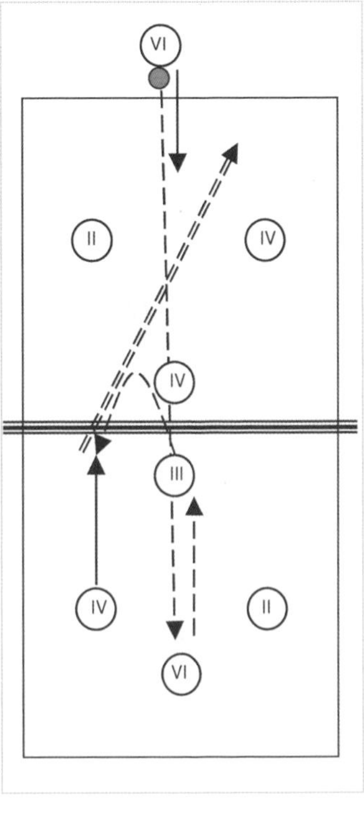

Fig. 58

Photo 79

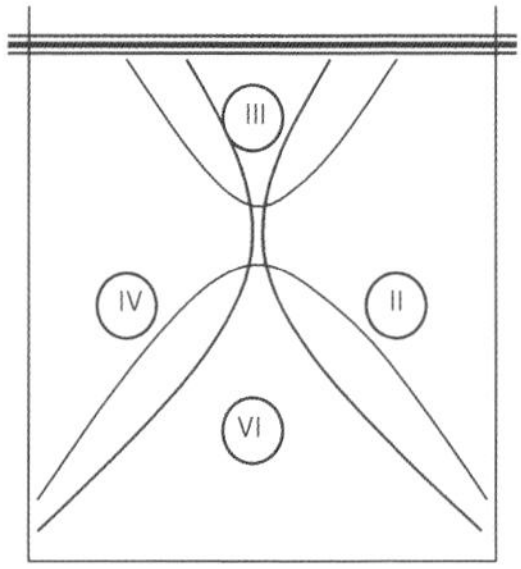

Fig. 59

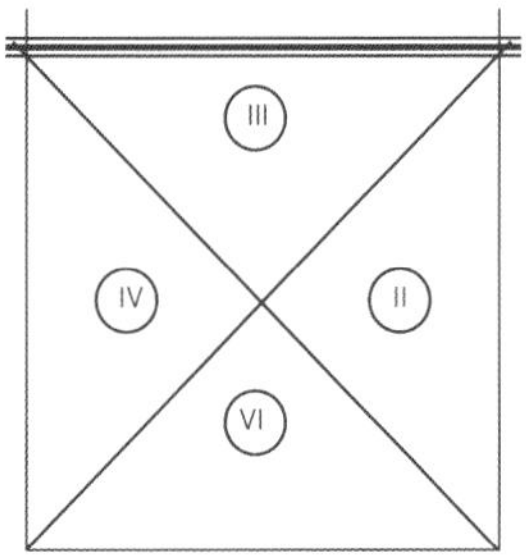

Fig. 60

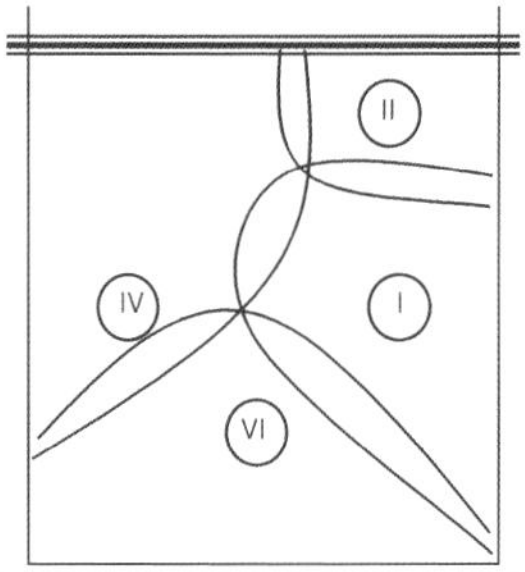

Fig. 61

The lines in fig. 59 help the players orient themselves with respect to their starting position in their formation. Fig. 60 shows the seam areas when receiving the ball.

However, the position-based attack build-up via pos. III can also be played without back-row players, meaning all four players act as front-row players.

For a ***position-based attack build-up*** via pos. II (fig. 61/62), the team can initially consist of two front-row players (pos. II and IV) and two back-row players (pos. I and VI).

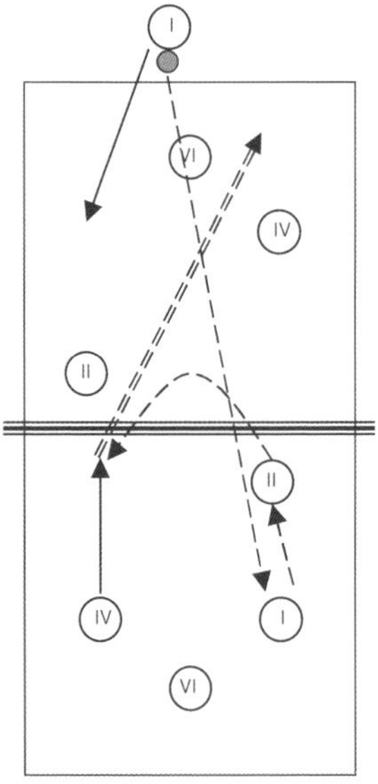

Fig. 62

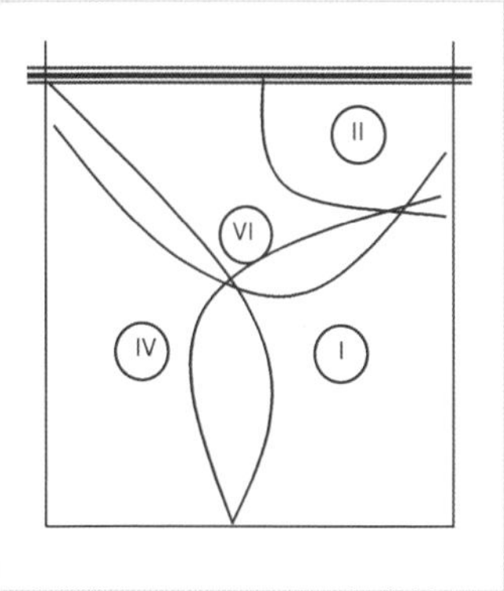

Fig. 63

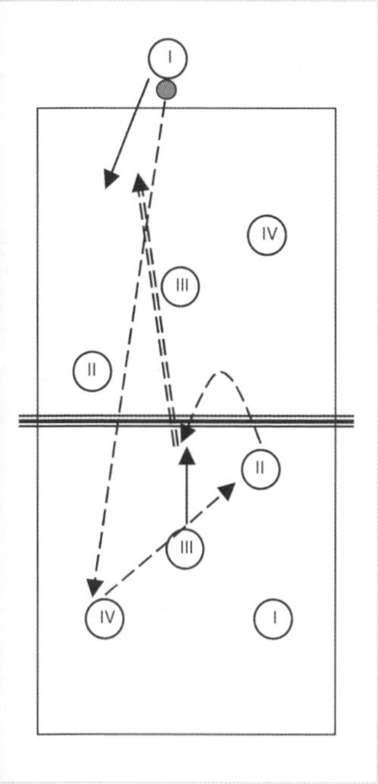

Fig. 64

The position-based attack build-up via pos. II can also be played without back-row players, meaning all four players act as front-row players (fig. 63/64). The transition from mini volleyball to midi volleyball also takes place with respect to the playing concept, meaning via the systematic game series. The game series are very similar to the systematic game series in mini volleyball, whereby the games used in midi volleyball should primarily be played with and against each other.

Hereinafter, ***methodological key aspects*** are identified within a game series for learning midi volleyball:

- Only catching and throwing the ball with each other.
- Only setting (and bumping) with each other.
- Underhand serve and shot/spin spike with each other.
- Only passing techniques against each other.
- Underhand serve and shot/spin spike against each other.
- Position-based attack build-up via the front-row player in pos. III with a three- or four-player defensive formation (main player pos. II, IV, VI; pos. III takes the short balls).

To learn the different serve-receive and defensive formations, the above systematic method must be implemented according to the following teaching priorities:

- Situation-based attack build-up via the front-row players in a four-player defensive formation (pos. II, IV, I, V).
- Position-based attack build-up via the front-row player in pos. III from a three- or four-player defensive formation (main player pos. II, IV, VI; pos. III takes the short balls).
- Position-based attack build-up via the front-row player in pos. II from a three- or four-player defensive formation (main player pos. III/VI, IV, I; pos. II takes the short balls).

In the same way as in mini volleyball, the ***midi volleyball*** players initially also play without the block, and with all four players playing defense. This is why we ***omit*** blocking from all illustrations. However, midi volleyball is extremely well suited to introducing group and team tactics. In particular, the ***spike*** (longer court) and the ***one-man block*** which is the most effective defensive technique against the spike, along with ***covering the attack*** can be taught. These additional basic techniques and their variations as well as the respective basic tactical formations are presented in ***Volleyball: A Handbook for Coaches and Players*** (Papageorgiou & Spitzley, 2006) and in the book ***Volleyball – Training & Coaching*** (Czimek & DVV 2017). The latter book was originally published in German, and the English version is scheduled to be released June 2021.

The game sport midi volleyball thus represents an essential intermediate stage or "bridge" between mini volleyball and the introduction of 6-on-6 volleyball, and the 0-0-6 system of play with six universal players.

Please note:
The following special rules make sense for youth divisions:

Age group U14 (age 13 and younger):

- For girls and boys, the net height is 2.15 m and the court dimensions are 7 x 7 m.
- The Portuguese (serving) rule continues to apply.
- Position changes are not allowed.
- Continuing to play a ball after it touched the ceiling is ***unfortunately*** no longer permitted.
- A team of four consists of three front-row players and one back-row player (server).
- The back-row player is not allowed to play the ball to the opponent above the top edge of the net.
- After receiving the opponent's serve, an attack must ***unfortunately*** be built up via the player in pos. III at the net. **Thus only a position-based attack build-up is allowed (which is inexplicable for methodological and didactical reasons!).**

4
Leverkusen
1
Volleyball

3 FROM MIDI VOLLEYBALL TO 6-ON-6

When teaching a technically sophisticated sport like volleyball, not only are the teacher's behavior and the choice of medium of critical importance, but most of all the ***methodological approach with a finely coordinated sequence of individual learning objectives***.

In this chapter, we will introduce a ***beginner-appropriate teaching model consisting of 17 learning objectives (see fig. 65)***. This concept takes into account the above-listed need for a sensible sequence of learning objectives. Here a learning objective is primarily achieved in two learning units. ***The first learning unit always builds the foundation for the second one***, meaning the first learning unit (LU) almost always refers to a technical element (or a variation) which is the basic requirement for the second learning unit. The second learning unit then focuses almost exclusively on learning a group or team-tactical formation, whereby aspects of individual tactics are always taken into account.

This realistic model is tried and proven particularly in the beginning instructions at school, as well as at the club level and in teacher/coach training. The most important basic aspects for a meaningful introduction and development of volleyball are addressed below for its successful implementation. Their consideration is essential to quickly achieving the cognitive motor component ***playing ability*** as well as the affective social components ***joy in playing/motivation*** (photo 80) and ***cooperation*** (photo 81).

Photo 80: Joy of playing

Photo 81: Cooperation

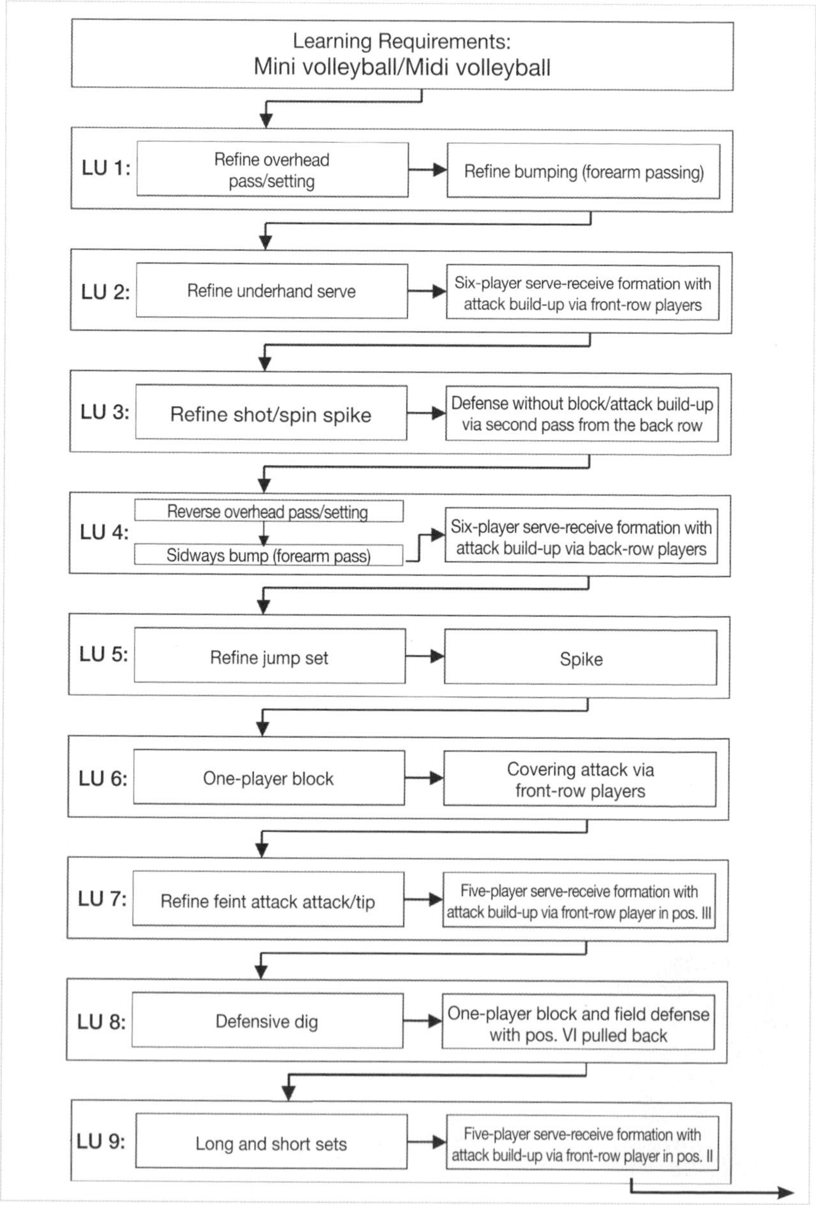
Learning Requirements:
Mini volleyball/Midi volleyball
LU 1:
Refine overhead pass/setting
Refine bumping (forearm passing)
LU 2:
Refine underhand serve
Six-player serve-receive formation with attack build-up via front-row players
LU 3:
Refine shot/spin spike
Defense without block/attack build-up via second pass from the back row
LU 4:
Reverse overhead pass/setting
Sidways bump (forearm pass)
Six-player serve-receive formation with attack build-up via back-row players
LU 5:
Refine jump set
Spike
LU 6:
One-player block
Covering attack via front-row players
LU 7:
Refine feint attack attack/tip
Five-player serve-receive formation with attack build-up via front-row player in pos. III
LU 8:
Defensive dig
One-player block and field defense with pos. VI pulled back
LU 9:
Long and short sets
Five-player serve-receive formation with attack build-up via front-row player in pos. II

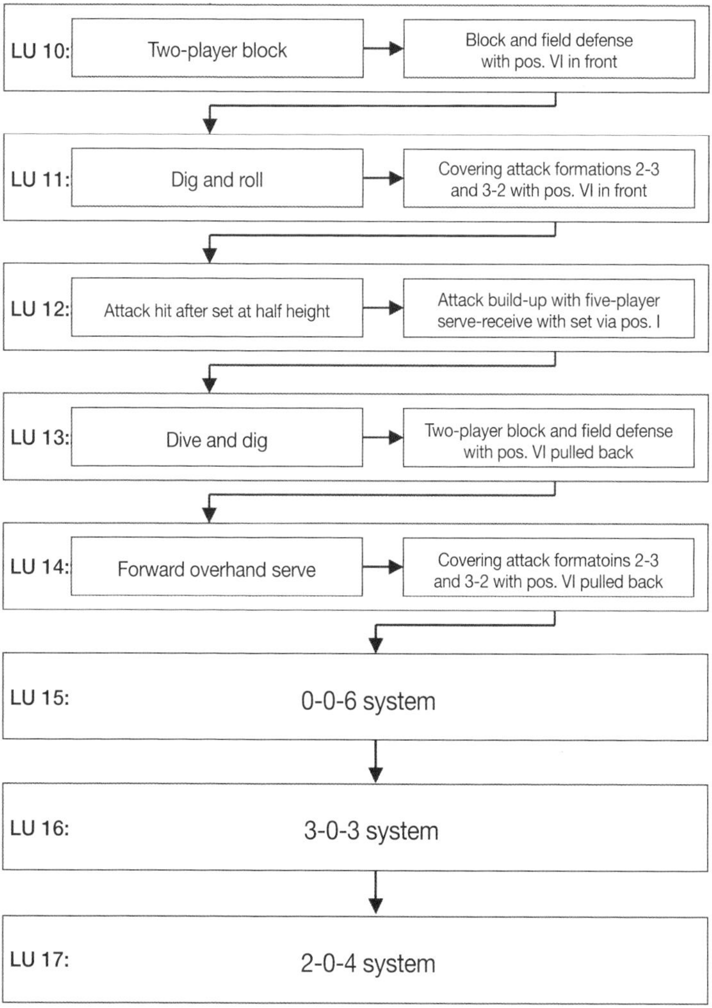

Fig. 65: Modified teaching model "From mini volleyball player to universal player" (as per Papageorgiou & Spitzley, 2005)

The main objective in introducing volleyball is to teach players to become ***universal players*** (fig. 65, learning objectives 1-15). The universal player must learn a wide range of individual, group, and team tactics and be able to use them in a game and a situation-appropriate way. This requires the ability to comprehend and implement the game's structure as well as all essential defensive and offensive interactions. To do so, the player needs to use his cognitive skills early on, be encouraged to anticipate movements, and learn to be flexible in his actions. ***Any kind of specialization should be distributed carefully*** during this stage of training in order to avoid prematurely limiting the player's development, but rather allowing him to achieve the highest possible degree of flexibility and as a result of this, creativity.

This insistence on amplified universal training is also supported by the rotation rule: it "prevents" a player from performing one-sided, overly specialized actions limited to only "offense" or "defense". ***Every volleyball player serves, receives, builds up, attacks, blocks, defends, and covers***. The libero as a receiving and defensive specialist or any other specialists (like for instance a fast attacker or diagonal attacker) should not be given any considered in beginning volleyball.

As in mini and midi volleyball, it is extremely important to continue to bring the students into ***situations in which they can choose their actions*** to ***initiate decision-making processes*** and promote volleyball as a game of movement. For this reason, the ***six-player serve-receive formation*** instead of the five-player serve-receive formation is the recommended formation as the first receiving formation on a full-size court, even if many volleyball experts to date have no experience with this formation.

For the reasons stated above, the 0-0-6 system of play should therefore be the first system used because it allows all players to equally experience and implement everything in all basic situations. The 0-0-6 system means that a team consists of six universal players that will receive, defend, pass, and attack (see fig. 65, learning objective 1-15).
But for those who do not want to start with the six-player serve-receive formation as the first formation, it is very much suggested to play only with a five-player serve-receive with attack build-up via the front-row player in pos. III until learning objective 7.

Particularly when introducing "6-on-6" volleyball, it is important to make sure that the receiving and defensive actions must be executed better or at least as well as the offensive actions.

For these reasons, the ***teaching concept*** starts with first improving the ***setting and bumping skills*** already learned in mini volleyball. Next they refine the ***underhand serve***. Since the overhand serve is very easy to learn but difficult to receive, it will only be addressed at the end of the concept.

The ***overhand pass from a jump*** as well as the shot/***spin spike*** are deliberately refined prior to the spike, which is considered the first true attack element. The movement sequences of both elements, particularly the approach and largely the timing, are a good preparation for the introduction of the ***spike***. The spike and block can already be introduced in midi volleyball if the players have the necessary playing skills.

Immediately after that, the ***one-man block*** and ***defensive dig*** are included in the learning process to practice the most important defensive elements against the spike. Once the ***longer forearm and overhead pass*** has been improved, ***players learn the attack build-up via the front-row player in pos. II***.

With respect to the ***block and field defense***, players start by playing with a ***one-man block formation with pulled back pos. VI*** (fig. 66) because the player next to the block must cover the block. Only with the introduction of the ***two-man block*** does the field defense initially play with a forward pos. VI (fig. 67), and later with the ***(two-man) block and field defense with pulled back pos. VI*** (fig. 68).

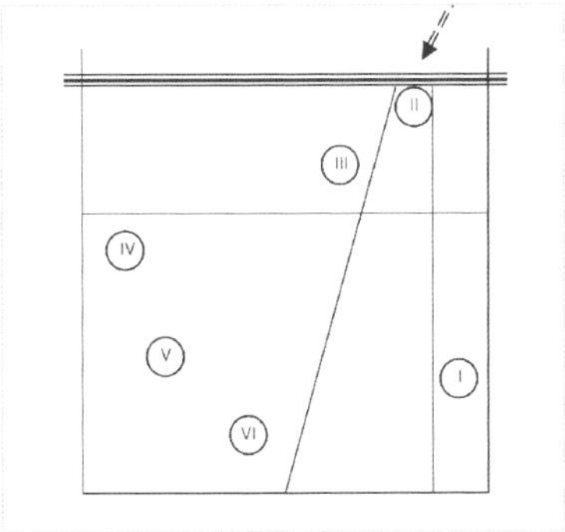

Fig. 66

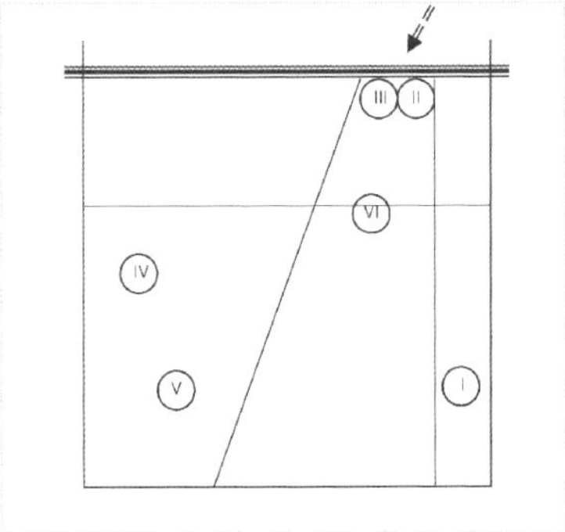

Fig. 67

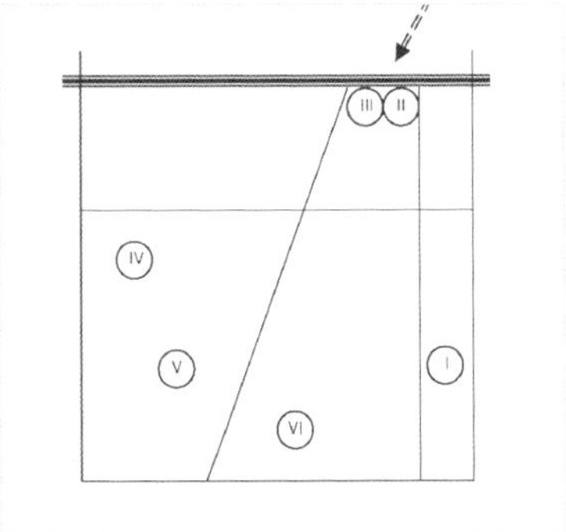

Fig. 68

Please note:

Exemplary youth division special rules listed here:

Age group U16 (age 15 and younger)

- For girls, the net height is 2.20 m and for the boys, it is 2.24 m; the court dimensions are 9 x 9 m.
- Volleyball game rules apply. However, use of a libero is not allowed.
- The Portuguese rule has been eliminated.

For **age group U18** (age 17 and younger), the U15 rules apply except for the net height (girls 2.24 m, boys 2.35 m), but the use of a libero is now permitted.

The **age group U20** (age 19 and younger) plays by adult volleyball rules without restrictions (net height for women 2.24 m, net height for men 2.43 m).

3.1 METHODICAL, DIDACTICAL, AND ORGANIZATIONAL AIDS

With respect to the following ***volleyball-specific teaching problems*** that frequently crop up when teaching volleyball, we present different, ***easy-to-use solutions/aids***, which will make playing more fun and help build skills more quickly.

Whenever there are ***major differences in the playing performance*** of students, the teacher should create teams equally with strong and weak players. Moreover, the scope of action of stronger players can be limited slightly with ***special rules*** (e.g. only attack with the weak hand) or they can take over ***key functions*** like, for instance, passing. ***Playing outnumbered*** (1-2, 2-3, 2-4, 2-6, 3-6, etc.) is also a way to balance differences in the players' performance level.

Decreasing the size of the court and/or raising the net is a way to ***prevent short plays*** by limiting the players' scope of action. Moreover offensive play can be mitigated with special rules (e.g. only shots/spin spikes) and defensive play can be simplified (e.g. double hits, catching the ball).

When ***lowering the intensity*** during class such as often happens in 6-on-6 play, it is good to take a step back to ***small court games*** and especially games ***"with each other"***, e.g. by also including volleyball-specific ***additional tasks***.

If the teacher ***lacks organizational resources*** in the gym (e.g. no net cross/lines for small court games), he can create additional courts with the use of ***magic cords/ tethers and elastic tape***. If there is an insufficient number of volleyballs, ***other balls*** can be used instead, or players can play chasing games and drills in which players ***switch functions*** like, for instance the triangle game with four or five players.

If problems surface during ***coeducational gym class***, the games, small court games, and competitive games should be played with a slanted net, whereby the girls will play at the lower end of the net. Another option is to play games on the ***girls' net***, whereby the ***boys can only attack with their weak hand*** or can only perform ***shots/ spin spikes***.

Other options in case of coeducation problems are to play games at the boys' net whereby the ***boys play the front-row positions and rotate among themselves, and the girls play the back-row positions and also rotate among themselves***. Games can also be played at the girls' net where ***the girls play the front-row positions*** and the boys play in the back.

3.2 METHODICAL SAMPLE SERIES

When transitioning from mini/midi volleyball to 6-on-6 play, students learn advanced techniques including their variations, for example the spike, the dive and dig, and the roll.

These techniques are coordinatively complex and difficult to learn and are taught over an extended period of time via methodical game series. We therefore introduce the ***methodical sample series*** below, which particularly emphasize the methodical steps.

During the transition from small court games to 6-on-6 play, the team-tactical positions should still be purposefully introduced and refined. Since the tactical formations have been very simple and easy to learn so far, we did not create a methodical series to teach them. However, the complex action sequences in volleyball require a ***methodical sample series*** for both the introduction and refinement of team-tactical formations.

3.2.1 SAMPLE GAME SERIES TO LEARN A TACTICAL FORMATION

First step: Create a mental image of the action

Any audiovisual means can be used to do this, whereby the mental image of the action must be created by communicating very few, important aspects.

It is further very beneficial to illustrate the image of an action by repeating the play by catching and throwing the ball. Here players should also learn to perform their movements in slow motion without the ball. Catching and throwing the ball quickly is also a recommended method for nailing down the formation players need to learn.

Second step: Play small court games with each other

Here part of the team (e.g. three players) play with each other on a small court in a formation that is appropriate for their tasks. It is best to start with 3-and-3 play before moving on to 4-and-4. When introducing individual tactical formations such as covering an attack, it is recommended to begin with 2-and-2 play.

Third step: Small court games against each other

The games with each other are now played against each other. Games played 2-on-2, 3-on-3, 4-on-4, and 5-on-5 should be played on different size courts to present the players with changing conditions.

Fourth step: 6-and-6 play

Here two teams of six play with each other with the goal that every player will be able to fulfill his function within a system of play by executing a technique with few problems.

Fifth step: 6-and-6 play or 6-on-6 play

First players perform three net crossings by playing with each other. After the third net crossing, players start to play against each other.

Sixth step: One-sided 3-on-6 play

In this game, three players have a supporting role to give the other players an opportunity to practice the formation they are learning in a near competitive setting.

When teaching some formations, 4-on-6 play is a good way to refine the formation that is being taught or make it more difficult. For organizational reasons, one-sided play can also be 1-on-6 or 2-on-6.

Seventh step: 6-on-6 play

Players play 6-on-6, whereby the teacher/coach can capture and analyze the implementation of the formations the students have learned.

Eighth step: Practice game

During the practice game (against another team/practice group), the teacher should purposefully observe the implementation of the learned tactical formations both casually and unsystematically, but also in a controlled and systematic way, in order to determine their applicability in a competitive game.

Ninth step: Competitive game

Here, too, but against equal opponents, the teacher/coach should observe, analyze, and discuss the implementation of the learned techniques (photo 82).

Photo 82: Discussing tactics before/after the game

3.2.2 SAMPLE DRILL SERIES TO LEARN A TECHNICAL ELEMENT

First step: Create a mental image of the movement

A mental image of a movement can be taught via explanations, drawings, videos, diagrams, etc. Here it is very important for the beginner to not be given a detailed explanation of the movement sequence, but no more than 2-3 main movement characteristics. Additional movement characteristics will then be added over the course of the practice series. It also includes all exercises performed with the use of aids (e.g. orientation lines for the correct execution of the pivot, lighter balls, etc.).

Second step: Practice under relaxed, easy conditions

This includes all exercises that are performed without a ball, by holding a ball, and by playing easy passes.

Third step: Simple complex drills

This includes exercises in which individual players perform ***only one element*** (e.g. the spike) in only one basic situation (e.g. attack). Here it makes sense to start out with a reduced number of players as well as a playing field/court.

Fourth step: Game-like, complex drills

This includes all exercises that give the beginner the opportunity to choose between two basic elements (e.g. spike or feint). This is initially done only in a game situation (e.g. receiving situation C1), later in both basic situations (meaning also from the defense situation C2). The beginner thus learns both the techniques' areas of application and the transition from offense to defense and vice versa. It is also best to first practice on a small court/field with fewer players gradually increasing the number of players and the size of the court/field.

Up to this step, this has been strictly a practice series, meaning we have only been using exercises whose application only makes sense for those very difficult playing techniques. In continued training, teachers should increasingly revert to games and competitive exercises as well as small court games with and against each other.

However, we must point out that ***games and competitive exercises*** are not only justified between the individual methodical steps of the practice series, but are a true ***asset to the teaching*** method. Of course this is also true in the reverse, particularly with respect to correction exercises.

The teacher/coach should occasionally insert ***monitoring exercises or games (incl. tests or learning stage assessments)*** when teaching an element, as well as during a tactical formation to determine whether the ***learning progress*** during the current step is sufficient to move on to the next methodical step, or the previous step must be repeated.

3.3 SYSTEMS OF PLAY FOR BEGINNERS

A system of play chosen in consideration of the players' athletic, technical-tactical, and mental skills defines the individual, group and team tactics. It represents a bundle of decisions made by the teacher or coach, the effectiveness of which is directly linked to how accurately the chosen system of play matches the skills of their own team, the opposing team, and any influencing variables that impact the game. ***Thus the system of play determines or rather encompasses position, area of responsibilities, range of functions and actions of individual players, the playing group and the entire team in the game's two basic situations.*** It should take into account the abilities of the opposing players and team in consideration of the strengths and weaknesses of their own players and team, in order to utilize their strengths and cover their weaknesses.

The system of play is listed in numbers whereby the first number refers to the number of ***setters***, the second number refers to the ***fast offensive players/middle blockers***, and the third number refers to the ***universal players/outside hitters***.

The following illustration and discussion about the individual systems of play refers ***only to the C1 situation (receiving formation with the respective attack build-up)***. The C2 situation (block and field defense situation with respective attack build-up) is not taken into account here as it depends primarily on the opposing team's abilities. ***All possible block and field defense information (forward or pulled back pos. VI with respective variations) can at any time be applied to every system of play.*** A detailed description can be found in ***Volleyball: A Handbook for Coaches and Players*** by Papageorgiou & Spitzley, 2006 and ***Volleyball – Training & Coaching*** by Czimek & DVV, to be released in 2021.

3.3.1 THE 0-0-6 SYSTEM WITH SIX-PLAYER SERVE-RECEIVE FORMATION

In the 0-0-6 system of play, every player acts as receiver, setter, attacker, blocker, and field defense player, which is why there are no position changes to strengthen the offense or defense. This means the team consists of ***six universal players*** and is therefore the simplest system of play. It can be used with beginners and advanced players during every phase or training, and is therefore the perfect beginning system of play in which the positions/defensive formations can be matched to the respective types of attack build-up and attack coverage.

The six-player formation (fig. 69/70) is the first receiving defensive formation introduced, because on the one hand it affords the ***best coverage of the entire court***, and on the other hand it already forces the beginning player to deal with ***situations that require decision-making and communication***. Moreover, it allows a variable attack build-up via the front-row players. The participation of all players in receiving the ball as well as variability in attack build-up, require and promote ***universal learning and development training*** because every player is prepared for every playing function and the decision of who will take on which function is only made during the respective game situation. The situation-based attack build-up thus promotes particularly the ***cognitive abilities of players and volleyball as a game of movement***.

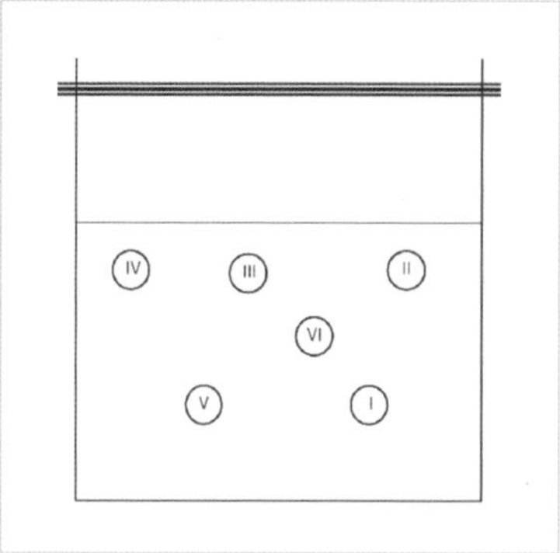

Fig. 69:
Six-player serve-receive formation

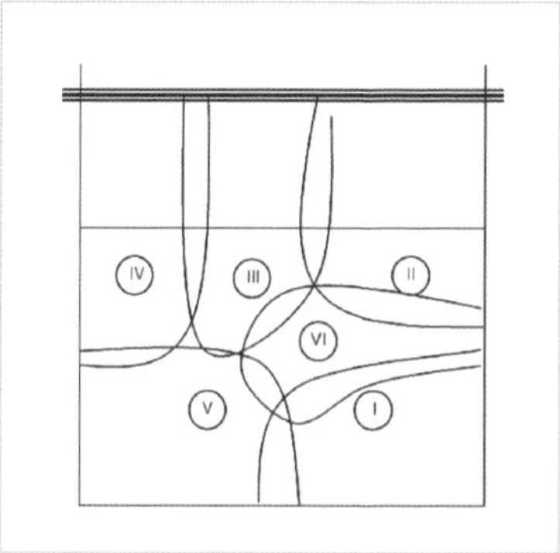

Fig. 70:
Seams in six-player serve-receive formation

Like all formations, the six-player receiving formation is used to receive and pass the serve. To do so, the players are positioned in a ***W-formation***, whereby the front-row players IV and III as well as II cover the entire front and middle of the court and are positioned equal distance from the server, approximately 1 m behind the attack line. The back-row players I and V cover the back of the court and stand approximately 2 m from the base line in the gaps between the front-row players. Player VI stands between players III and I and covers a portion of the middle of the court. Player III is positioned slightly closer to the player in position IV.

Since all players participate in receiving the serve, the ***attack build-up is situation-based with a six-player receiving formation with players being able to move around freely in an open-game situation***. As in mini volleyball with a three-player formation, the decision of who sets the ball from which position depends on where the ball is received:

When the ball is served to receiving are IV, V, and III, meaning into court-half A (fig. 71), the front-row player II runs to the net to set the ball. When the ball is served into receiving area II, I, and VI, meaning court-half B, front-row player IV sets the ball (fig. 72). If a first pass is too short, player III (or another player) can help out.

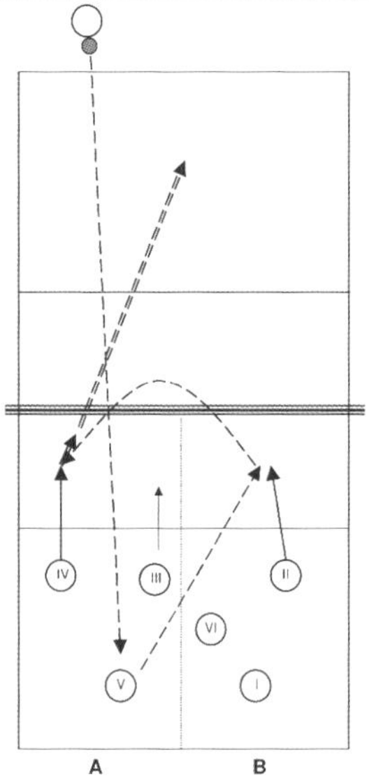

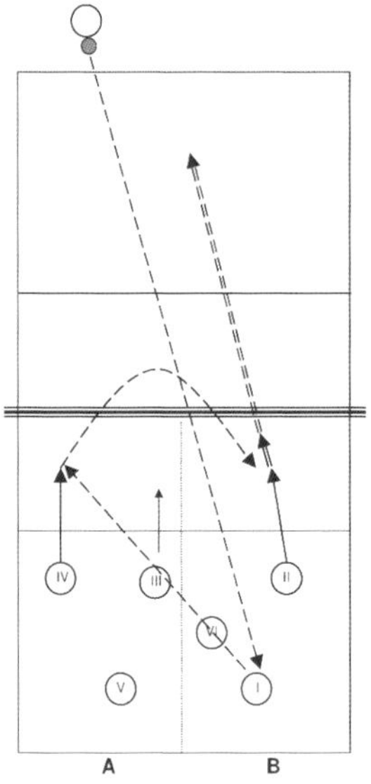

Fig. 71/72: Attack build-up with a six-player serve-receive formation

A fundamental rule is that the ball should always be received high and diagonally, not too close to the net and the ball should always be set high, frontally and parallel to the net.

Recommended actions:

- Always watch the server's stance and movement prior to serving the ball to be able to ascertain the ball's trajectory.
- Watch the ball's trajectory and speed for early recognition of the receiving location.
- As a receiving player, make a timely decision on whether you will receive the ball or move to the net as the setter.
- If necessary, use verbal communication with the player(s) next to you.
- When you are going to receive a high and slow-moving ball, choose to set the ball because in this situation a double-hit is permitted.
- After a game interruption, quickly move back to your receiving position in the formation and coordinate with the players next to you.
- As the server, keep an eye on the players in a six-player defensive formation and take advantage of any mistakes.

3.3.2 THE 0-0-6 SYSTEM WITH FIVE-PLAYER SERVE-RECEIVE FORMATION AND ONE SETTER IN POS. III

The five-player formation (fig. 73/74) is a serve-receive formation in which five players cover the field in a ***W-formation***. The sixth player (pos. III) has left the formation to be able to exclusively prepare to set the ball in pos. III in the front zone at the net. Thus the receiving and passing of the ball to the setter in pos. III is a ***position-based*** play. The setter in pos. III will then play an overhand pass parallel to the net, forward or backwards if this skill has been learned, to the attackers in pos. IV or II (fig. 75). ***The position-based attack build-up via pos. III means that every player in pos. III will set the ball.*** This is not considered an ongoing specialization of players, which is why it is also referred to as a variation of the 0-0-6 system of play.

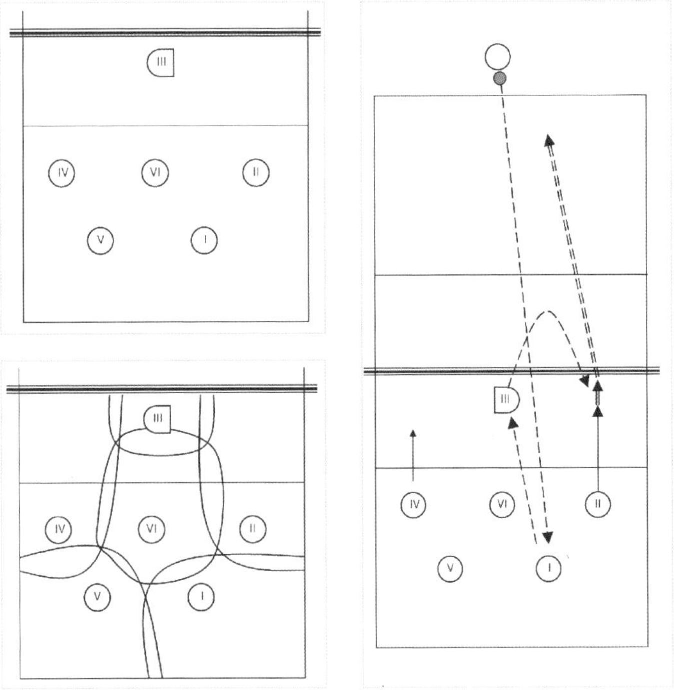

Fig. 73-75: Five-player serve-receive W-formation

In a five-player formation, the front-row players (pos. IV, VI, and II) cover the entire front and middle of the court. They all stand at approximately equal distance from the server, about 1 m behind the attack line. The back-row players (pos. I and V) cover the back of the court and stand about 2 m from the baseline in the gaps between their front-row players. Together with the front-row players and the player in pos. VI their formation looks like two triangles of equal size (W-formation). Pos. VI moves up into the front receiving row and takes over player III's receiving area.

The principle that balls played into the seams should be received by the player that is moving toward the setter, and thus is able to pass the ball ideally frontally in running direction, applies specifically to the position-based attack build-up. He should verbally announce his intention to receive the ball.

The setter at the net should position himself (right shoulder to the net) so he can see the server and the formation and does not block his teammate's view of the server. He should stand ***at least 1 m from the net*** so the received ball, if it is played too far forward, does not travel directly over the net but the setter can still get to it, thereby avoiding consequential errors.

3.3.3 THE 0-0-6 SYSTEM WITH FIVE-PLAYER SERVE-RECEIVE AND ONE SETTER IN POS. II

The five-player formation with attack build-up via front-row player II (fig. 76) is an expanded position-based attack build-up. ***Here, every player in pos. II acts as the setter and leaves the formation.*** The back-row player I directly behind setter II operating at the net moves into the front-row receiving line and takes over player II's receiving area. Back-row player VI in turn takes over the receiving area in pos. I.

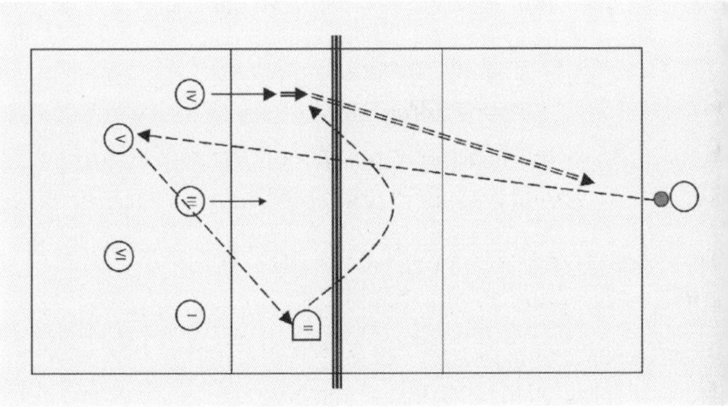

Fig. 76: Five-player serve-receive formation with attack build-up via pos. II

Compared to the attack build-up via pos. III, the attack build-up via pos. II with a five-player serve-receive formation makes higher technical and tactical demands on the players, because the ***distances the ball travels***, both in receiving and passing as well as setting, ***are longer*** (almost more than 7 m). The reasonable use of this type of attack build-up requires mastery of accurate, long diagonal and parallel passes.

If the requirements mentioned above have been met, the attack build-up via pos. II offers the following ***advantages***:

- The setter has a good view of the server, receiver, and attacker and thus can employ reasonable individual tactics.
- Frontal passes can be made to both attackers/hitters and right-handers can be used advantageously from the hitting side.
- It is easier for the setter to watch the opponents' behavior, particularly the blockers.

But the ***disadvantage***—particularly if the first pass is imprecise—is that the opposing players can generally recognize the attack position early, allowing the blockers to easily form a two-man block. This is also made easier because in these situations, players are not yet able to utilize the entire width of the net for the attack.

For the following reasons, it makes sense to ***introduce the attack build-up via the front-row player in pos. III first***:

- The setter in pos. III is in a central location and approximately equal distance from all the receiving players.
- The receiving players have to turn very little to receive a ball set from pos. III.
- The setter in pos. III only has to play short or medium-length passes.
- The setter in pos. III has to run shorter distances.
- Due to his central position, it is easier for the setter in pos. III to balance out imprecise first passes.

During the position-based attack build-up, the receiving players must still be ready to set imprecise first passes themselves as they already learned in the six-player defensive formation, after communicating with the setter.

3.3.4 THE 3-0-3 SYSTEM

The transition from universal play to specialization should take place in small increments. No differentiation and thus specialization should initially take place in receiving, attacking, or blocking field-defense situations, but rather only in the area of attack build-up when a ball has been received (C1). Situation- and position-based attack build-up gradually changes to an individual-based attack build-up. This is done by introducing the 3-0-3 system of play with ***three setters and three universal players BEFORE*** introducing the 2-0-4 system of play.

The method used to transition from 0-0-6 to 3-0-3 is simple. Three of the six universal players act as setters and each is assigned to one attacker/universal player (fig. 77/78).

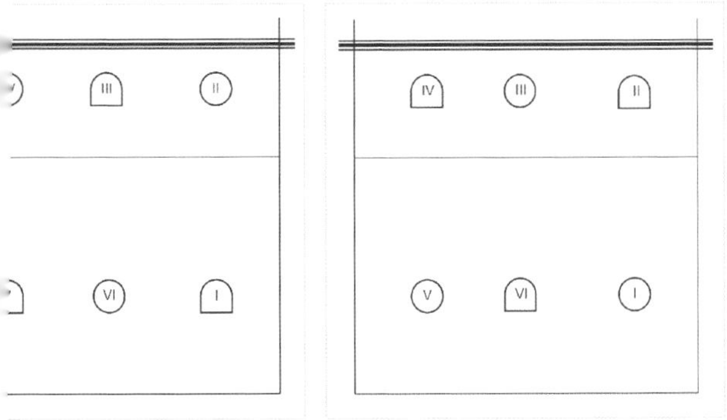

Fig. 77/78: Positioning setters and universal players in the 3-0-3 system of play

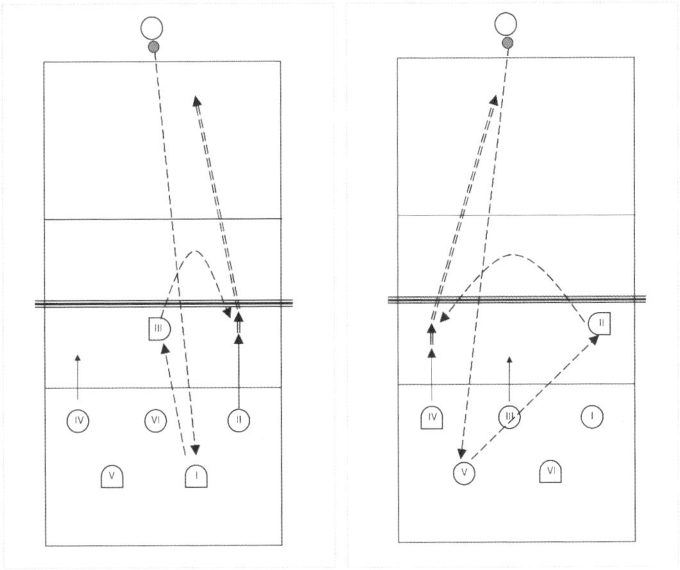

Fig. 79/80

The 3-0-3 system of play is also well suited for beginning specialization because it can initially be played without position changes. If one of the three setters is in pos. III, players play a five-player defense with attack-buildup via pos. III in the C1 situation (fig. 79). If the same setter is in pos. II after the subsequent rotation, the attack build-up again takes place with a five-player defense via pos. II (fig. 80), meaning each of the three setters only plays when he is in pos. III or II.

3.4 ADVANCED SYSTEMS OF PLAY

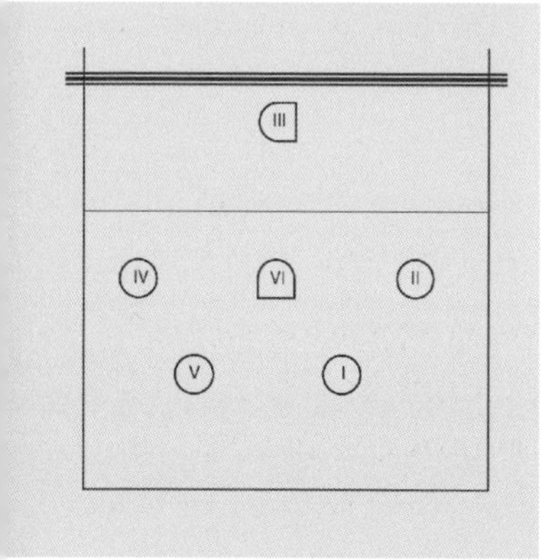

The ***2-0-4 system of play*** is another step towards specialization. Here ***two players act as setters*** that are positioned diagonally across from each other in the basic formation, and ***four players act as universal players/attackers*** (fig. 81). When assigning positions to the universal players, it is important to position two players with similar qualities diagonally across from each other. This ensures nearly equally strong front and back rows through all six rotations.

Fig. 81: 2-0-4 system of play with setters in pos. III/Vi

Expansion of, or rather increased effectiveness of the systems of play, is achieved by introducing or executing ***position changes***. This is not only possible when introducing the 2-0-4 system of play, but essential. The position changes make it possible to optimally utilize players according to their abilities in a ***permanent front-row or back-row position***. In doing so, the changes primarily serve to strengthen the defense during their own serve and secondly to support the attack build-up. The changes during the opponent's serve primarily strengthen setting and hitting.

During all position changes, it is essential that the receiving performance does not suffer.

The illustrations and explanations of the systems of play focus primarily on the changes during the opposing team's serve. However, changes made during their own serve are also reflected in the illustrations.

If the team plays with a forward VI, the setter in the back-row always changes to the forward pos. VI. If the team plays with pos. VI pulled back, the back-row setter changes to pos. I. The back-row setter additionally acts as an assisting setter, meaning he should set the ball after an imprecise first serve-receive or defensive pass.

3.4.1 THE 2-0-4 SYSTEM WITH SETTER IN POS. III

Like the 3-0-3 system of play, the 2-0-4 system of play is initially taught with only ***short position changes***. After receiving the ball in a five-player defensive formation, here the attack is always built via the setter in pos. III.

If the setters are in pos. III and VI, the attack is built via the setter in pos. III (fig. 82). If the setters are in pos. II and V, setter II changes to pos. III and acts as setter (fig 83).

This results in a change to the five-player formation. Player III handles the serve-receive in the right front half of the court so he can attack via pos. II, without having to run a longer distance. Here the ***positioning guideline*** must always be observed.

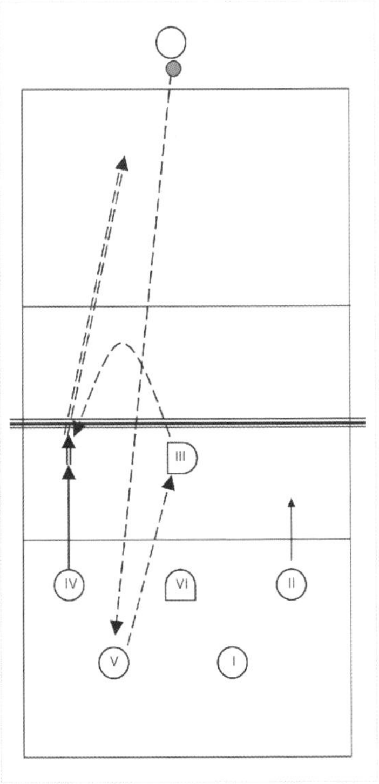

Fig. 82

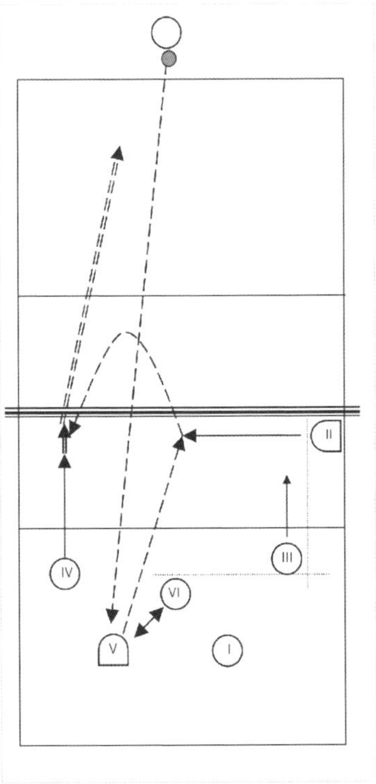

Fig. 83

This means that ***every front-row player must always stand in front of the back-row player directly behind him, and to the left or right of the player immediately next to him, before the ball can be served (fig. 84)***.

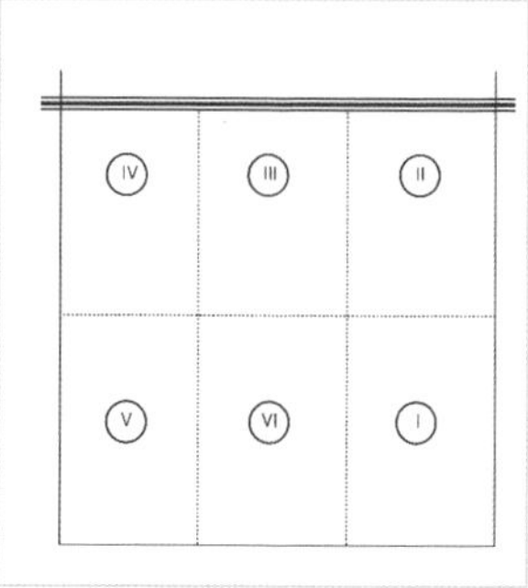

Fig. 84 Layout for the positioning rule

With respect to the above-mentioned formation, this means that in the receiving formation, the universal player in pos. III must stand to the left of the setter in pos. II and in front of the player directly behind him (pos. VI). Immediately after the serve, the setter in pos. II moves to pos. III to act as setter there, and the attacker/universal player in pos. III has already moved to his offensive position II.

To ***avoid positioning errors***, the following principle applies:
The back-row player VI is responsible for positioning errors with pos. III. The front-row player III is responsible for errors with the setter II or IV. The setter is not allowed to stand outside the court or walk/run to the setting position before the serve is played. The ***position changes of back-row players*** take place after the ball has been received or the attack has been covered. If their own team serves, all players choose their starting position according to the shortest-distance principle (fig. 85).

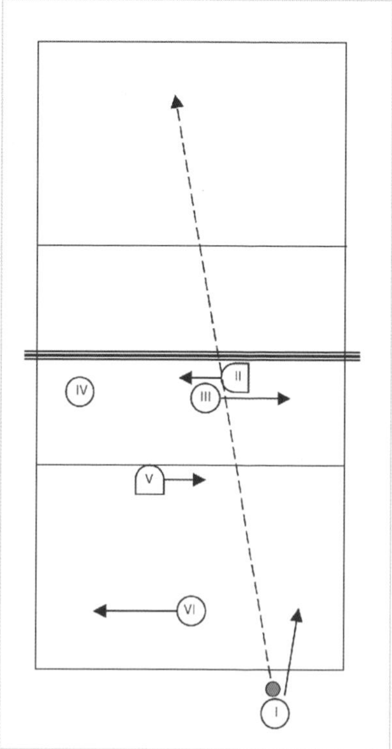

Fig. 85: Changing positions by own serve with player on pos. VI forward (setter II/V)

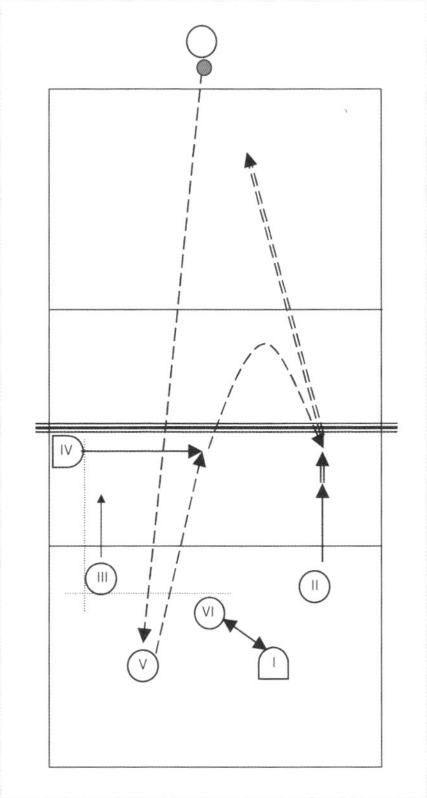

Fig. 86: Opposing team serve and own team change positions with pos. VI forward (setter IV/I)

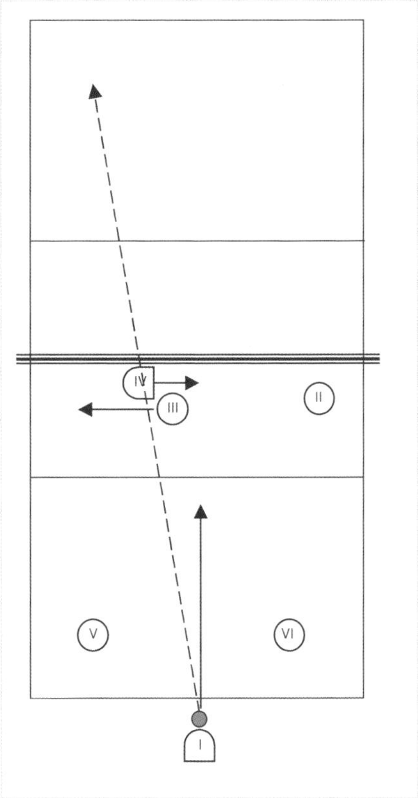

Fig. 87: Changing positions by own serve with player on pos. VI forward (setter IV/I)

If the setters are in pos. IV and I, the attack-buildup takes place in mirror reverse (fig. 86).

Principle: The player in pos. VI takes over the receiving area of player III during all six rotations. This provides the players with an orientation aid so that they are able to get into their defensive formation quickly and accurately.

3.4.2 THE 2-0-4 SYSTEM WITH SETTER IN POS. II

As previously mentioned, for beginners it is easier to build their attack via pos. III instead of pos. II. The transition to the 2-0-4 system of play with the setter in pos. II requires the players/beginners to be able to particularly set and dig (receiving and defending) with precision over longer distances.

With respect to tactics, the 2-0-4 system of play with the setter in pos. II results in many new team-tactical receiving formations that require a lot of playing intelligence in terms of player synergy.

When the setters are in pos. III and VI, the attacker in pos. II takes over player III's front and middle receiving area. This shifts the receiving areas of players VI and I as shown in fig. 88.

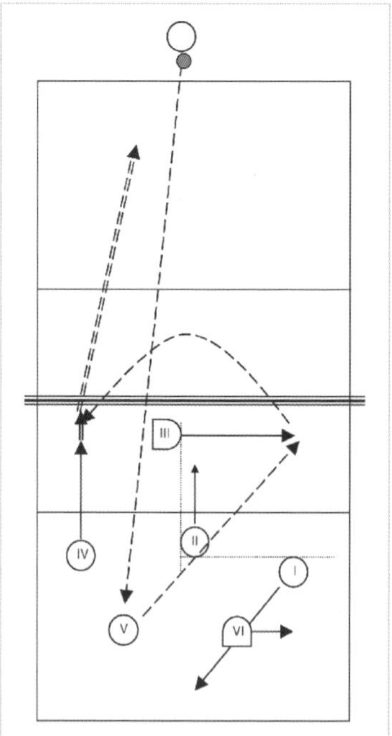

Fig. 88

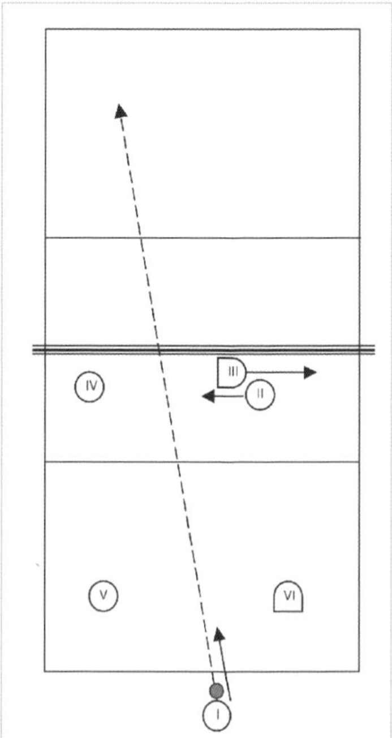

Fig 89

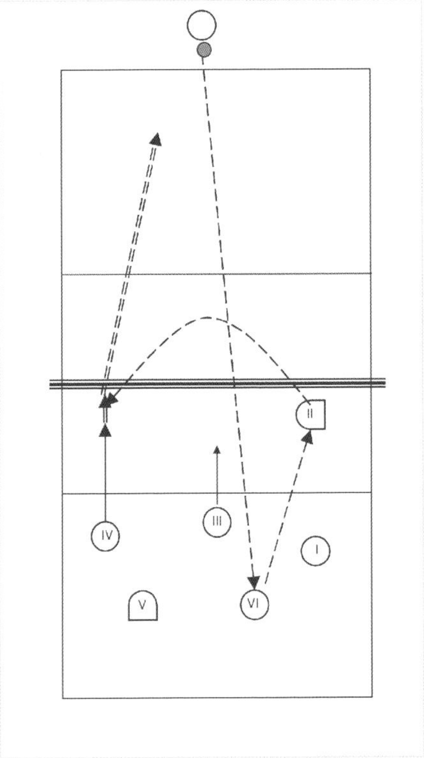

Fig. 90

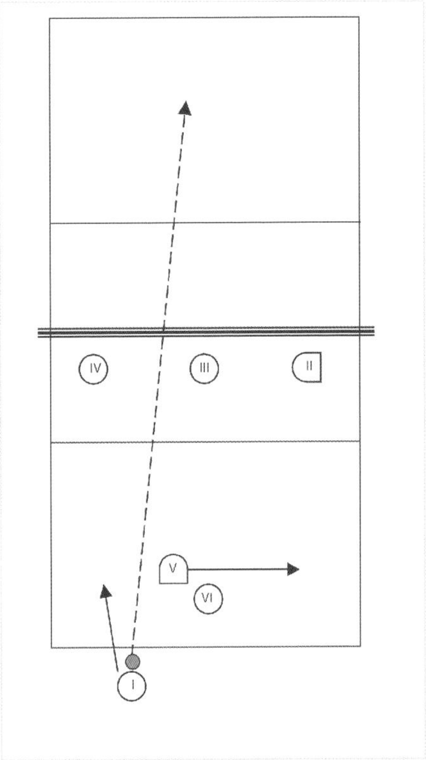

Fig 91

Fig. 89 shows the position changes during their own-team serve with block- and field defense with the pos. VI pulled back. When the setters are in pos. II and V, the formation during the opposing team's serve looks like fig. 90. During their own team's serve, it should look like fig. 91

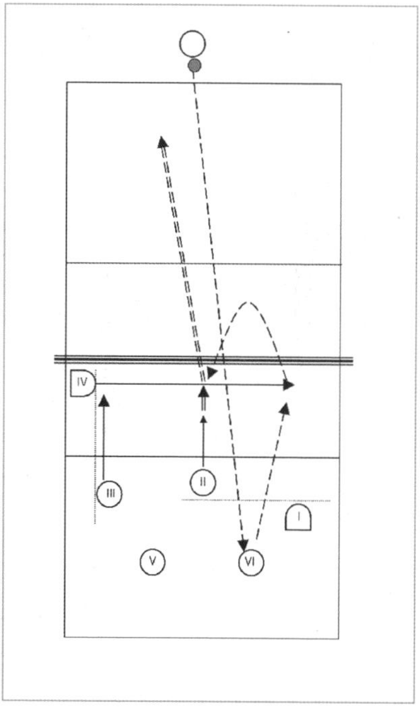

Fig. 92

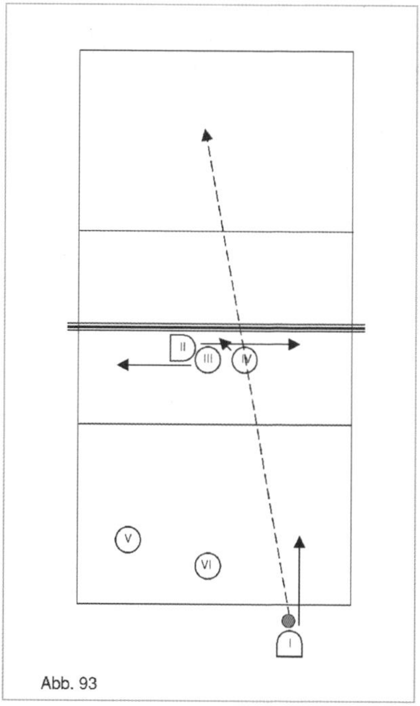

Fig. 93

When the setters are in pos. IV and I, the front-row players III and II as well as the back-row players VI and I, assume the receiving positions and areas shown in fig. 92.

Guideline: The player in pos. I takes over the receiving area of front-row player II during all six rotations. This provides the players with an orientation aid so they are able to get into their defensive formation quickly and accurately.

Fig. 93 shows the formation during the own team's serve.

BIBLIOGRAPHY

Barth, K. & Heuchert, R. (2005). *Ich lerne Volleyball.* Aachen: Meyer & Meyer.

Barth, K. & Linkerhand, A. (2006). *Ich trainiere Volleyball.* Aachen: Meyer & Meyer.

Czimek, J. & DVV (Hrsg.), (2017). *Volleyball – Training & Coaching. Vom Jugend- zum Leistungsvolleyballer. Kombinierte Rahmentrainingskonzeption Volleyball und Beach-Volleyball des Deutschen Volleyball-Verbandes.* Aachen: Meyer & Meyer.

Döbler, E. & Döbler, H. (2003). *Kleine Spiele. Das Standardwerk für Ausbildung und Praxis* (22. Aufl.). München: Südwest.

Dietrich, K., Dürrwächter, G. & Schaller, H.-J. (1999). *Die großen Spiele* (5. Aufl.). Aachen: Meyer & Meyer.

Graef, M. (2006). *Spielen und Gestalten* (unveröffentlichtes Manuskript).

Meier, M. & Nussbaum, P. (1994). *Volleyball für Kinder. Ein Lehrmittel für Trainer -innen und Lehrer/-innen.* Stans: Schweizerischer Volleyballverband.

Papageorgiou, A. & Czimek, V. (2002). Didaktische Überlegungen zur Ein- und Weiterführung des Volleyballspiels. In G. Treutlein (Hrsg.), *Lehren und Lernen in Sport und Sportunterricht.* Festschrift für Fritz Dannenmann (S. 71-79). Idstein: Schulz-Kirchner.

Papageorgiou, A. & Spitzley, W. (2005). *Handbuch für Volleyball.* Grundlagenausbildung (7. Aufl.). Aachen: Meyer & Meyer.

Papageorgiou, A. & Spitzley, W. (2002). *Volleyball. A Handbook for Coaches and Players.* (engl. Ausgabe des Handbuchs für Volleyball. Grundlagenausbildung.). Aachen: Meyer & Meyer.

Papageorgiou, A. & Wilberg, J.-O. (2003). *Hinführung zum Mini-Beachvolleyball und Mini-Hallenvolleyball* (unveröffentlichtes Manuskript).

Papageorgiou, A., Krapp, L., Wilberg, J.-O., Koch, T. & Naffin, R. (2005). *Beach Volley meets school.* Broschüre der deutschen Volleyball-Jugend für Sportlehrer/innen zur Vermittlung des Beachvolleyballspiels in der Schule (2. neu überarbeitete Aufl.). Frankfurt: Deutsche Volleyball-Jugend.

Voigt, H.-F. & Richter, E. (1991). *Betreuen – Fördern – Fordern*. Münster: Philippka.

Zalewski, W. (1995). *Spielen vor dem Üben. Vielseitig-zielgerichtet. Von volleyball-orientierter zur volleyballspezifischen Spielfähigkeit*. Dortmund: WVV.

CREDITS

Cover design: Andreas Reuel

Interior design: Katerina Georgieva

Layout: Guido Maetzing, www.mmedia-agentur.de

Cover photo: © Shutterstock

Interior photos: Robert Kampczyk (photographer)
Photo series 60: Detlef Gottwald
Photos 46 b and c: Martin Miser

Figures: © Dr. Jimmy Czimek and Athanasios Papagorgiou

Managing editor: Elizabeth Evans

Copyeditor: Qurratulain Zaheer